# Mindfulness Workbook

Relieve Stress and Anxiety and Sustain Peace and Happiness

(How To Fight Addiction and Cure Anxiety through Meditation)

**James Long**

Published by Rob Miles

© **James Long**

All Rights Reserved

*Mindfulness Workbook: Relieve Stress and Anxiety and Sustain Peace and Happiness (How To Fight Addiction and Cure Anxiety through Meditation)*

ISBN 978-1-990084-10-2

All rights reserved. No part of this guide may be reproduced in any form without permission in writing from the publisher except in the case of brief quotations embodied in critical articles or reviews.

## Legal & Disclaimer

The information contained in this book is not designed to replace or take the place of any form of medicine or professional medical advice. The information in this book has been provided for educational and entertainment purposes only.

The information contained in this book has been compiled from sources deemed reliable, and it is accurate to the best of the Author's knowledge; however, the Author cannot guarantee its accuracy and validity and cannot be held liable for any errors or omissions. Changes are periodically made to this book. You must consult your doctor or get professional medical advice before using any of the suggested remedies, techniques, or information in this book.

Upon using the information contained in this book, you agree to hold harmless the Author from and against any damages, costs, and expenses, including any legal fees potentially resulting from the application of any of the information provided by this guide. This disclaimer applies to any damages or injury caused by the use and application, whether directly or indirectly, of any advice or information presented, whether for breach of contract, tort, negligence, personal injury, criminal intent, or under any other cause of action.

You agree to accept all risks of using the information presented inside this book. You need to consult a professional medical practitioner in order to ensure you are both able and healthy enough to participate in this program.

## Table of Contents

INTRODUCTION .................................................................. 1

CHAPTER 1: WHY LOOK FOR A WAY OUT? ......................... 4

CHAPTER 2: BUILDING BLOCKS ......................................... 18

CHAPTER 3. EXPLAIN THE SCIENCE OF THE MINDFUL BRAIN ............................................................................................ 22

CHAPTER 4: HOW TO HARNESS THE POWER OF YOUR MIND ................................................................................. 31

CHAPTER 5: MINDFULNESS MEDITATION ......................... 48

CHAPTER 6: ADVANCED STEPS IN MINDFULNESS ............ 53

CHAPTER 7: MINDFULNESS AND CBT FOR IMPROVING YOUR MINDSET ................................................................ 59

CHAPTER 8: THE BUBBLE AROUND US ............................. 72

CHAPTER 9: BASICS OF MINDFULNESS MEDITATION ....... 77

CHAPTER 10: WHY PEOPLE FIND MINDFULLNESS AT WORK ADVANTAGEOUS ............................................................. 97

CHAPTER 11: BOOSTING RESILIENCE .............................. 101

CHAPTER 12: HOW TO MANAGE THOUGHTS TO CONTROL ANXIETY ......................................................................... 108

**CHAPTER 13: OBSTACLES TO MINDFULNESS AND HOW TO GET OVER THEM** ............................................................ 136

**CHAPTER 14: DIFFERENT TYPES OF MEDITATION** .......... 142

**CHAPTER 15: 21 DAYS ACTION PLAN TO GAIN MINDFULNESS** ............................................................... 151

**CHAPTER 16: FORGIVENESS** ........................................... 160

**CHAPTER 17: SIMPLIFY YOUR WORK** ............................. 165

**CHAPTER 18: MINDFULNESS FOR EMPOWERMENT** ....... 172

**CHAPTER 19: BEGINNING MEDITATION** ......................... 180

**CHAPTER 20: MINDFULNESS TIPS AND HACKS** .............. 184

**CONCLUSION** ................................................................ 189

## Introduction

Practicing mindfulness has become very popular though it isn't a new concept. Practiced, perhaps in a very different way by Buddhist Monks for centuries, mindfulness simply means being aware of the moment in which you are living. That may sound a little like hugging trees or learning mantras to you, but you would be wrong. Mindfulness means that you are able to come to terms with problems, overcome depression, build upon your self-consciousness and become happier.

Your life improves vastly by practicing mindfulness and the exercises throughout this book will show you, in uncomplicated terms, how you can apply mindfulness to your life. Does it mean joining classes? Not necessarily. Some people are able to manage the exercises needed on their own and are happy to do this.

So what's different about this book? The book takes a refreshingly new approach to mindfulness and puts it in simple terms for those who have never thought of it before and who are unaware of all the technical terms and details usually used by professionals. The problem with the professional stance is that it forgets that the target audience may never have practiced mindfulness in their lives and will thus become lost in a maze of instructions that mean very little to them.

This book goes back to grass roots. It explains what you are doing and why you are doing it. It shows you how distant you are from living up to your ideal and demonstrates your inability to achieve happiness and why it's happening to you. That's something that has been gleaned from experience but without jumping into technicalities which make for boring reading.

This book was written for those seeking peace within their hectic lives and shows techniques that can be practiced by anyone. That includes you. Why was it written? The book was written because mindfulness has opened the doors to the author to a life which is happy and which is in harmony. Was my life always like that? If it was, there would be little to write about. My life was hectic, going through all of the motions of handling a career, looking after the welfare of kids and moving from one country to another. In the process of emotional turmoil and unease, mindfulness allowed me to find my peace of mind and true contentedness that has lasted many years. Now, it's your turn to discover the benefits of mindfulness for yourself.

## Chapter 1: Why Look For A Way Out?

An optimist and a pessimist met.
Pessimist:
- Worse will not be.
Optimist (joyfully):
- Yes, it will be! Will be!
Did you hear it too? This eternal call. Spiritual teachers, gurus, and other mentors call us on the road. Who is in heaven, who is in Nirvana, who is in the promised land. And despite the fact that something like that always responds to us inside us, at the same time, I want to ask why?
What is wrong in life, since you have to go somewhere, do something, change somehow? What is wrong with us if there are so many proposals for "improving yourself"?
After all, most of us are fine - there is work, money, family, and various technical innovations. Sometimes, however, not

everything is good - it happens that there is no work, no money, no modern toys. And if everything is "just so bad," then, we prefer not to pay attention to it. We close our eyes to sensations and feelings, a breakthrough from morning to evening through the shroud of everyday life. Then go to sleep and find some peace in oblivion. And the need to change something in yourself is minimal, if not absent.

We sometimes live actively, live by the Internet, career, business, travel, shopping, caring for homeless cats or dogs, skiing or cycling, parties. Someone lives studying others, saying: "There they are, there, so-and-so, but we are still nothing, still normal, still holding ourselves." Someone goes further and slips into a pool of dependencies on substances, people, and circumstances.

Why? Yes, because deep down, we know something is wrong. We hide and suppress this knowledge, but it does not go anywhere, it remains with us, from time to time gently but firmly tapping the shoulder, reminding of itself. The call is heard. We dismiss him, but it is impossible to dismiss ourselves.

Sometimes everything is really good. We meet a wonderful person, get a good job, buy a new car, go to watch an excellent movie, win the lottery, make a willful decision to go on a diet or play a sport. When life is easier, we even start to think: "Finally! Now everything will be fine, and I will be happy. "

Time passes, and the euphoria of the first moments go away, the novelty of change fades, and on the threshold, our old acquaintance appears - discontent. Suddenly everything is gray again, familiar, boring. The usual dull reality of every day worries.

We again think that something is wrong with us. Someone bold goes to specialists, talks about these strange states. Someone prescribed medication, herbs, or pills —

something to sleep, something to wake up. In the evening, we drink, sleeping pills to sleep, and in the morning, we ingest caffeine in order to stay awake. Someone closes his eyes, being convinced that no "experts" will help.

We follow the advice of glossy magazines and learn to be positive and smile no matter what. Our motto: "The best way to overcome problems is to decide that there are no problems."

And then we go further in our simple struggle with ourselves. We are creating a universe called "here if." Now, if I buy a house, now, if I get a job, or if I conclude this deal, but if I buy this car or write this book. But if I go to the islands or if I lose weight. If only they loved me. We live in a permanent desire to run away. We are committed to the future, driven by the idea of "here if." We are not enough of what is in the present. We need more. On the other hand, it is possible that for some reason we don't want to be in the present, we don't want to be with ourselves, with reality.

We are building a whole culture to maintain the general illusion that everything is in order, the industry of distractions from ourselves, from a quiet inner voice, timidly telling us: "No, not everything is in order." What for? We want to reach a certain point, after which we will no longer need to achieve anything. We want to know for sure. Be calm. We believe that this is exactly what the desired will bring us-happiness. And in life, it is not stable. It is constantly changing. It does not stop, do not enter into a clear and understandable framework.

Buddha, as we remember, walked around India and said that life is suffering. Then his followers went, someone even reached the edge of the world, came back and told us about suffering. Suffering? But why is this all of a sudden? Somehow very pessimistic. Are there no moments of happiness in life? The first kiss, for example, or the confidence that the person you like also thinks about you, or the impressions during that trip to the islands, or the birth of a child.

However, if you look closely at them, remember how it really was. Every "happy moment" has a shadow side. We feel it well. We want to hide it, close it. That is why we memorize these moments, take pictures or videos. And then we tell, try to relive, trying to make these moments continue so that they do not end. On your wedding day, things do not always go as planned. There might be, constant stress, total control over each episode, nerves, something was not brought, someone did not come, someone had a fight, or something was broken. On the islands, maybe you were burned in the sun, had problems with documents, or you ran out of money.

It seems that this is a big part of the problem; everything goes away. Another part of the problem is that often, in an effort to remember and capture these events, we drop out of them. So much that later, we have to revise everything and "re-live" because, at the time, when all this happened, we were anywhere, but not "there" and not "then."

What then is happiness?

If we start from external manifestations, it turns out that happiness lies in the possibility of having everything we want, or a little more. On the other hand, true happiness, according to the most frequently encountered version, consists in the possibility of complete control over what is happening. We believe that then we can finally relax.

The need for control is a very important component of potential happiness. Control over the world, people, circumstances is a must. To all was ours how we want it. To "they" behaved correctly. They spoke correctly. They did the right thing. How exactly "right," we define, based on our own beliefs and ideas.

That's right; this is when I do not care what is happening. When the world is stable and does not change. And therefore, the sad truth is that control is impossible because stability means nothing less than death. Life is a constant change. Birth, growth, maturity, extinction, care.

We know that. And we fight it. We do everything to win. And the victory is impossible, and we suffer from the eternal struggle for stability, from the eternal defeat in a hopeless battle with nature. We build pyramids, skyscrapers, create stabilization funds, perform many different, sometimes quite funny acts in the framework of this struggle.

The problem is that all our actions and our decisions are directed outward. Outward, there, where everything is shaky. Where there is no genuine stability, for any material, it is subject to destruction.

I moved to California in the hope that my ancient dream of the promised land is realized, and I will find peace in my soul. And how could it be otherwise? This is America. Moreover, this is Los Angeles! It is a city of eternal sun, golden sunsets, a fresh, cool ocean, a dream factory, and a conveyor of sweet tales about an easy and carefree life.

At first, everything was as it was. Everything was new, amazing, delightful. Unnoticed, drop by drop, quietly, but stubbornly boring stones of past ideas, life began to sneak up. I remember well the day when I walked home along the avenue. The gentle winter sun was shining, but it was cool enough for a walk. It was Saturday, I went after an excellent workout in a new and clean gym, and everything was fine at home. My beloved wife was waiting; there was great food; there were stability and confidence.

All in all, everything you could dream of. Suddenly, quite unexpectedly for me, as if jumping out from around the corner, the good old feeling returned. Something felt missing. Ashamed - how can you? Discouraging - what more could you want?! Frightening - if such a reality does not please, then something is clearly wrong with me. I am bad or afflicted with some kind of terrible and abnormal disease. I'm confused.

I began to look for the answer - what is wrong? I must admit that I knew the answer. I just did not want to recognize it, because knowledge imposes a great responsibility. Responsibility for the right search. Search not outside, but inside.

The answer to the question of where to find happiness is that you need to look inside. And not because there is hidden stability or lack of change, but because it is within yourself that you can quickly find something that is not outside. Something real, authentic, true.

I am a man. I feel what many people around me feel. Anxiety, insecurity, and dissatisfaction. And these are normal feelings. You can't understand without them that you need to change something, do something, act somehow. These feelings are markers, lighthouses, which say: "The path is not finished, keep moving!" You don't have to run away from them.

And so, when different ones were tried (perhaps, practically all external ways of solving internal problems), at first an absolutely wild thought comes: "Maybe the inner should be corrected by the inner? But how?"How to stop fighting with yourself? It turned out that there is a remedy. It is simple and long known. This is meditation. The goal of meditation is personal transformation.

The one who starts the meditation and the one who finishes it is not identical personalities. There is a change. Meditation changes the mind and character of a person. It improves attentiveness, increases awareness regarding thoughts, words, and actions. Resistance to the events of the external world decreases, the ego recedes into the background, the mind calms down, comes to a state of equilibrium and life. With respect to life, the struggle goes away; there is a feeling of gliding over it. And all this is due to the meaningfulness in the life developed by meditation.

If we were to express what meditation is in three words, these three words would be concentration, attentiveness, and weakness.

Together, these qualities form the foundation of a happy and peaceful life. Just the fact that is so actively sought.

Today I begin my day with meditation. For me, this is part of my morning routine. Meditation is my half an hour of hygiene and mind gymnastics. It is necessary to purify not only the body but also the consciousness. Brush not only your teeth but your mind. To develop not only the body with the help of simulators but also the mind with the help of meditation.

Peace brings freedom from anxiety and distraction, gives the opportunity to respond to current events more adequately. The mind becomes sharper, the ability to concentrate develops, and the understanding of the principles of the internal mechanisms of consciousness deepens.

Another by-product of meditation is the development of intuition. Seeing the true nature of things without prejudice and illusion becomes much easier.

In the process of meditation often come different great ideas, the right decisions are born, new perspectives open up in seemingly simple and banal situations.

The most important thing is that it becomes much more comfortable to be in the present moment. You can stop so desperately needing various "distractors," such as social networks, news programs, shopping, games, food, care gadgets, or, as we like to say, "just to relax, get distracted." "Distractions" cease to dominate attention, disappearing by themselves, as something unnecessary. It turns out that it is easy to start enjoying what is here and now. And do not go around half the world or even the whole world in search of an unknown elusive condition for finding peace. All you need is to sit down. Close your eyes. Start the practice. Check everything yourself.

## Chapter 2: Building Blocks

Everything we have looked at so far is part of the building blocks that take us to meditation and beyond. How do you recognize that you are in a state of being mindful?

It is not a mere coincidence that I brought up breathing as the first example and the first exercise that you will perform among many other exercises in this book. Breathing is the essence of life, and just like we are the conduit between abstract and reality, our being is the conduit between what is here and now and what is everywhere else in space and time.

Our mind is divided into two. The first part is the consciousness we are aware of. The second part is the subconscious that we get glimpses of sometimes. Just as we are this conduit between imagination and reality, our minds too are the conduit between the present moment in time and space, and everything else.

When you compare the present moment in time and space to everything else, the present moment it minuscule. It is the same without conscious and subconscious. Our conscious is tiny in comparison to our subconscious.

The problem arises when we try to take everything we experience and let our conscious sort it out. It is not built for that. When you try to plan the future, think about the past. Analyze past actions and pile on everything that is not from this moment in time and located in this point in space, onto this tiny part of our mind, it breaks down. When the conscious breaks down, it manifests itself in mental degradation; reduce physical health, unhappiness and everything else that is wrong in our lives.

This is why mindfulness is the single most important tool to fix everything in our lives.

Mindfulness allocates the present moment in time and space to the consciousness without trying to take on any other burdens. When that happens, the subconscious kicks in and starts to take care of everything else. This is how we are built and this is exactly what we need to navigate this universe.

When this happens, the resources are aligned with the surrounding. The consciousness manages the here and now and is not overwhelmed. Health returns, clarity of mind returns, and the person generally turns the corner and begins to enjoy the life this universe has to offer. At the same time, the individual's subconscious is keeping an eye on other places in space and points in time and constantly dictating what we need to do to keep everything in harmony.

This is the essence of peace - a cosmic harmony that pervades us at a very deep level and knowing everything is as it should be. This can only be achieved through mindfulness and meditation. Now that we know what it does and what it looks like, now let's get started with how we can get started with mindfulness and meditation.

## Chapter 3. Explain The Science Of The Mindful Brain

The progression from Buddha to a doctor in Worcester, Massachusetts to media giants promoting mindfulness is important because the practice, in fact, the need for being present, is the fundamental building block of everything we care about. Making the world a better place, feeling happy, performing well on ordinary days and under pressure: what we hope for is only possible if we are mindful first.

But our modern minds still need empirical evidence to believe a lifestyle change is good for us. Where mindfulness used to be considered fringe, esoteric or ethereal, scientists in the field of neurology and psychology now consider it proven. And when we can explain the science of mindfulness, we no longer have an excuse not to practice.

The technology that revealed the brain's mindful powers is called functional magnetic resonance imaging (fMRI). In the early 1990s, originally with mice and then with people, scientists plotted the amount of blood flowing to different parts of the brain.

The brain doesn't produce its own glucose, the gasoline that runs our body. When a part of the brain needs energy to operate, more blood flows to that region. More blood means more neural activity. Scientists realized they could show the difference between an image of a brain that was quiet and one that was active based on blood flow.

Up until 2000, hundreds of studies were done using the new technology to capture brain functions like attention, perception, language, and memory. What engaged different regions of the brain was catalogued in the same way the first mapmakers in ancient Greece charted the world.

Then, in 2001 at the University of Washington, St. Louis, Marcus Raichle put participants in a fMRI machine. He gave them no assignment. He wanted to see what happened to the brain when people had nothing in particular to focus on. With a focus on something to do, a collection of brain regions known as the extrinsic network light up. When subjects became bored, this extrinsic network went dark. Unexpectedly, a second network filled the scientists' screens.

About the same time in Madison, Wisconsin, Richard Davidson was bringing to life an idea that began with the Dalai Lama. In 1992, the Dalai Lama challenged Davidson, an expert in the neurology of emotions. He asked the professor to bring the same scientific rigor he used to chart negative experiences like depression to positive states like happiness and compassion.

Davidson performed fMRI studies on highly-trained monks, those who had meditated for more than 10,000 hours over decades. He found something extraordinary. He saw the regions of the brain responsible for happiness and compassion turn on.

So he tested his theories on the value of meditation with the monks and a group of volunteers. Instead of measuring which part of the brain brightened, he measured for gamma waves. Gamma waves are the electrical sign that neurons are communicating. The theory is that with more connected neural pathways, compassion and happiness ensue. While the volunteers who were new to meditation could only produce a fraction of the monk's neural electricity, they too could exhibit the signs of a brain prone to happiness after just weeks of practice. This is where the science starts to inspire our practice. Practice more, Davidson proves, your brain gets happier.

It gets better. Since 2008 Zoran Josipovic, a practicing meditator himself, has also been scanning the brains of Buddhist monks. Just as the DNA of a person who is genetically immune to a virus can help researchers develop a cure, the brains of monks are the obvious lynchpin to discovering ways for each of us to find greater mental health.

The intrinsic network is the part of the brain that turns on when we reflect. These regions produce our auto-biographical memory and our creativity. Josipovic took the 2001 study in which bored subjects turned on their intrinsic network to a startling new frontier.

Just like the monks in Davidson's studies, Josipovic's 20 monks and nuns had more neural communication. Now, pause for a second. What you're about to read may be the holy grail of the life waiting for all of us if we choose.

The NYU monks and nuns were able to keep both their intrinsic and extrinsic networks on at the same time.

While Davidson's work shows that we can change our brains to be happier, Josipovic's work reveals that we are not only at the whim of our circumstances. What happens to us does not have to be the sole determining factor of which brain regions activate. If we experience trauma, the timeline to recovery varies from person to person, but we can heal. You may not be able to stop a panic attack, but the research now shows that with practice you can recover quicker. Painful experiences and mental illness are no longer the end of the story.

The NYU research uncovers the exciting possibility that with enough intentional practice, we can be present to both the outside world and our inner lives at the same time. Instead of melting down when things don't go our way, we can see every experience as learning. In the middle of our best days, we are able to share that joy with others rather than merely getting high on our own good fortune. Societal problems become the catalyst for new discoveries. A relational conflict becomes the spark of deeper understanding and the love and friendship that follows. Our brains are no longer either/or organs reacting to our circumstances or feelings: they are the control panel we can use to dive into entirely new realities.

The benefits and practicality of total mindfulness became even more apparent in the research of Amishi Jha from the University of Miami. In 2010, she taught marines to meditate. The goal was to help them improve attention and working memory on the battlefield. The Department of Defense and the Veterans Administration also want troops to be more resilient in handling the inevitable post-traumatic stress of war.

Her study reveals that twelve continuous minutes of meditation daily is the dose needed to keep soldiers focused on the present rather than past worries or future concerns. The study also showed that for soldiers who meditated less or didn't meditate at all, their focus actually decreased. Twelve minutes of mindfulness seems like a tiny investment to improve our quality of life.

And the value of mindfulness can also be experienced even more quickly. Another study at the University of Wisconsin-Madison had participants look at highly negative scenes. These caused the alarm in participants' brains to ignite. Yet when they reappraised the scenes unemotionally, meaning they reframed the images without negativity, the alarm calmed down and the prefrontal regions responsible for focus kicked in. Just changing the meaning of an experience turns down our stress response and the negative emotions that come with stress.

The summary of all these the findings is inspiring. With mindfulness practice, our neural pathways stay open. Our different networks communicate. The part of our brain that causes us to feel stress quiets down. With a little meditation we can pay better attention and have superior memory. We can literally slow, transform, or negate the permanent damage of negative emotion by intentionally reframing. The question now is not whether we should practice, but how.

**Chapter 4: How To Harness The Power Of Your Mind**

Many people think that mindfulness is meditation. You can practice mindfulness in different ways. All you need to do is to focus your whole attention on it and you can attain a mindfulness exercise. You can stop with the simple exercise of mindful eating or just deep breathing.

You can also follow short guided meditations. You can listen to audio tapes to help you focus. But meditation is not the only way to attain mindfulness. You can also notice, eat, listen, touch or just travel mindfully. You can practice mindfulness while simply lying down or playing a game.

It is not about multi-tasking, rather being fully present in the moment and whatever you are doing. It is about cherishing the moment with all your mind, observing everything around you without judgment.

Find what feels right for you! As Jon Kabat-Zinn said, "It's about living your life as if it really mattered, moment by moment by moment."

Start with making mindfulness a part of your daily routine to maximize the benefits of this healing tradition. Even a few minutes spent regularly can help you to cultivate mental awareness and help you attain a healthy body-mind balance. Very simply, just start your day with a one-minute or five-minutes of meditation.

Whenever you have time during the day repeat it. During lunch try to practice mindful eating. Try to practice focusing on a simple object in your office and slowly feel the peace within you. For healthcare professionals, deep breathing exercises or meditation can help create the benevolent environment for the patients.

You can also practice mindfulness when you're traveling through mindful observation. Empty your mind and let the calm enthrall your body and mind. If you face emotions, let it surge. There's nothing wrong with facing your emotions but conquering it with time is equally important.

In the 1970s, Professor Jon Kabat-Zinn developed a mindfulness-based stress reduction (MBSR) program that uses mindfulness practices to help people fight different issues with life. This program was developed at the University of Massachusetts Medical Center. This program uses various practices such as mindfulness meditation, yoga, body awareness, etc.

Today mindfulness practices are used to treat patients with various disorders, particularly depression. Mindfulness-based cognitive therapy (MBCT)is a kind of psychotherapy to help prevent relapses in depressive patients. Patients who practiced mindfulness meditation for 45 minutes a day, for eight weeks found changes in their symptoms of depression.

Even though mindfulness originated from Buddhism, with its deep roots in spiritual teachings, mindfulness practices have nothing to do with religion itself. It is secular. Over the last three decades, studies have shown that people who practice mindfulness regularly have noticed a sense of well-being, improved relationships, better focus, and concentration, better ability to handle their emotions, and overall increased happiness and capacity to enjoy their life.

Some of the practices that you can use to cultivate mindfulness are:

Mindful Breathing

Spend a couple of minutes to feel your breath. Practice mindful breathing with your eyes closed. Stop everything that you're doing. You can do it even at your office desk. Just detach yourself from your surroundings. Concentrate on your breath as you inhale and exhale. Calm your mind. Don't get frustrated if you are flooded with distractive thoughts.

The best way to let go is by doing nothing. Let the thoughts flood in. Let your emotions pour out. Do nothing. The lesser you resist, the better you will learn to go with the flow. Slowly detach with every thought or emotion that is conquering over the moment. Keep breathing. Pay close attention to your breath. It is normal to take a few weeks to calm down.

Start breathing. Breathe in. Breathe out. One breath cycle should last for 6 seconds. The best way is to inhale from your nose and exhale from your mouth. Let the breath flow throughout your body. You will notice that with every breath your thoughts too rise and fall.

Watch your breath as it will help you to focus and make you more aware of your body as it fills you up with life. You may think that you are not capable of meditating but if you have done this exercise once, you can do it again. Keep trying till you start to feel your senses surrender to the tranquility hidden deep within, and around.

Mindful breathing is the most common meditative practice practiced by many spiritual traditions Book in the East and the West. To start off, try to sit for 10 to 15 minutes every morning or night.

Once you gradually start to develop this as a habit, continue for at least 2 to 3 weeks before you try any other mindfulness practice. No matter what you practice try to always include formal sitting meditation and mindful breathing every day. This will always be the base for mindfulness no matter what your skill level is in the future. The secret to attaining mindfulness is going slow. Do not rush. Then you will gain nothing from your practice. Make it a routine like brushing your teeth. Choose a particular time every day. It does not have to be the exact time every day but follows the routine, maybe once in the morning, during lunch and before you go to bed.

Find a quiet place so you can focus without distractions around you. Feel comfortable with what you are wearing or how you are sitting.

There are different forms of meditation but sitting meditation in a quiet, distraction-free zone, is by far the most common one. Any other kind of meditation where you're not sitting is a much more difficult practice for a beginner.

Once you learn to make your mind quiet you can try other forms of meditation too. Always remember, that no matter how good an athlete is, he has to practice the fun.

Mindful Seeing

Mindful observation is simply seeing what is in front of you and savoring the moment while observing it. Simple observations such as your dog lying down on your favorite pillow, or your cat bathing in the sun. It may not be significant but seeing something so clearly helps you to live and enjoy the moment. Just notice how the sunset affects the color of the buildings.

Note how the sky changes its colors as it turns from day to dusk to the night. Watch the moon as you bathe in its fading light. It sounds insignificant but enjoying what's right in front of you without any distraction will help you be more mindful. You may be seeing another event that is playing within your mind while you are also seeing what's before you.

Your mind's eye is always seeing something else. Our mind is so fast that at one point in time you may be experiencing more than two competing visuals. Try to detach from these internal dialogues and emotions and just focus on clear seeing. Focus only on what's in front of you at that moment. Don't judge what's ahead of you, instead just accept the world around you with its beauty and imperfections. Relax your mind. Choose any object that stands before you in watch it for a minute or two. Don't do anything apart from just observing the object. Observe the object as though you are seeing it for the first time.

Savor the object, explore and enjoy every aspect of this object. Let the presence of the object consume you. Try to connect with its energy as it dissipates into the surroundings. Mindful seeing and increase your capacity for self-control and self-awareness.

Mindful seeing can help you to widen your perspective. Just being able to see clearly as a truly joyful experience. Even when you are just driving down a road, just look at the beautiful trees and try to appreciate the most beautiful tree on your way. Even though you take the same road every day, try to look with fresh eyes.

When you look at something you do it by choice, but how do you choose to look at it can be a source of mindfulness. As John Berger said, "We only see what we look at. To look is an act of choice. As a result of this act, what we see is brought within our reach – to touch something is to situate oneself in relation to it. We never look at one thing; we are always looking at the relation between things and ourselves."

Mindful Listening

You can practice mindfulness with everyday sounds in your life. The simple way to start mindful listening is by listening to your own breath. When you sit down to meditate, try to use a bell to start or end a meditating session. You can also use an app on your phone to help you focus on meditating.

A familiar sound can help filter out other distractions and help us to be consumed by the sound around us completely. Try to attune your mind to a sound and try to focus constantly. Don't get swayed by internal thoughts or dialogues of the past, or of the future. Hearing is not listening.

You need to start listening so you don't miss the present moment. Listen to the sounds of life like the wind blowing, the rustling of the leaves, the rain pouring on your window sill, the cacophony of the birds in your garden, the rhythmic beating of the heart when you place your ears against your partner's chest, the whistle of the train in the middle of the night.

When you start to listen, you become more aware of your surroundings and of the present moment.

You can practice meditation by selecting any music from the radio that does not associate with any painful experience from your past. Now close your eyes. Don't judge the music or the artist.

Just savor the sound and the music and lose yourself during the duration of the song. Enjoy the music. Make yourself aware of the beat and dance to the music. Immerse yourself by trying to separate each sound from another in your mind. You should focus on the sound completely, without judging the lyrics, the composer, the artist or the instruments. While you hear, do not think.

Mindful Empathy & Appreciation

To experience or show appreciation or gratitude is a prerequisite for Mindfulness. You appreciate a glass of cold, juicy mango juice on a hot summer day. You drink it loving every sip of it, savor the taste and the texture. You not only practice mindful eating in this way but also reap the benefits of the juice because you have it with complete focus and mindfulness.

When you experience something good, you should appreciate it from the core of your body, mind, and soul. Feel it. Use your senses to appreciate it. Appreciation is powerful because you make a valuable connection with the person or that thing. When a job is well done, appreciate the person doing it. Everyone loves being appreciated. Just acknowledging the presence of someone who made a difference in your life, is powerful.

It makes a difference even to the person whose job you appreciated. Appreciate the moment of mindful presence, the emotion, and the feeling, and express it when you experience it. Even if it's an unknown voice or an unfamiliar face, take a moment to smile and let them know that you acknowledge their presence.

It is the presence of the person or thing at that moment that has touched you, so appreciate the moment and the reason behind it.

When you start to practice mindfulness, you will start to loosen up. You will start to feel for others. You will experience moments of empathy for your fellow human beings in distress. Science proves that compassion and empathy activate different networks of the brain.

Mindfulness can help improve relationships and develop compassion for others. You can identify with other's pain and may have the capacity to help them. Once you start to value others, without judging them, you can start to love. When more people start being empathetic, it will lead to a cohesive society.

There will be a sense of togetherness and looking out for each other during difficult times. As Dalai Lama said, "If you want others to be happy, practice compassion. If you want to be happy, practice compassion."

Mindful Awareness

Mindful awareness helps to build self-awareness, strengthen relationships, build tolerance, promote self-control and regulation, and reduce anxiety. The more you practice mindful awareness, the better you will be aware of what is and what isn't. The best way to achieve mindful awareness is in the lotus position, with eyes closed, and by practicing meditation.

The idea is to discover more even while performing the same tasks every day. Even when you are watering your garden, pay attention to every detail of that task. Awareness occurs with the discovery of mindfulness. Imagine you go to a garden and notice a beautiful rose.

Mindfulness is discovering this rose in the garden but the choice to bring it home with you is awareness. While you are mindful, you also need to be aware of everything around you because based on that you need to make decisions that may be life-changing.

Mindfulness and awareness work hand-in-hand to help you accept and embrace situations as they are. While mindfulness keeps you in the moment, awareness helps you to make choices in that moment. The journey of meditation happens with the combination of these two attributes.

By doing this, you are essentially practicing the quality of paying attention over and over again. It helps change the way how we relate to our own feelings and that paramount for self-growth

Finally, do what you love and do it with all your focus and attention. Whatever it is, be all there. Our mind has a set routine of thinking, doing and feeling. Once you improve your awareness and consciousness by practicing mindfulness, you will start making sense of every task you do, even on a daily basis like washing our clothes, showering and cleaning the house.

Mindfulness slows down the process of feeling, thinking and doing by engaging all your senses and making you fully aware of your present moment. Once you start performing your daily tasks with your complete focus, it will enable you to pave your way towards overall well-being of your body, mind, and soul. Start off with being kind to yourself and consistently practice mindfulness on a regular basis and see the changes in your persona and life.

As Thich Nhat Hanh said, "Feelings, whether of compassion or irritation, should be welcomed, recognized, and treated on an absolutely equal basis; because both are ourselves. The tangerine I am eating is me. The mustard greens I am planting are me. I plant with all my heart and mind. I clean this teapot with the kind of attention I would have were, I giving the baby Buddha or Jesus a bath. Nothing should be treated more carefully than anything else. In mindfulness, compassion, irritation, mustard green plant, and teapot yeah are all sacred."

## Chapter 5: Mindfulness Meditation

Before you complete this exercise, I want you to try to visit somewhere natural that inspires you at sunrise or sunset – it might be a beach, or by a river in a forest, or perhaps even as basic as a nearby park. The reason being that there are times of the day when you are very inspired by what you see and can celebrate it in a certain amount of peace and tranquility. As you look over this sight that awes you, you feel a certain sense of smallness – a sense of humility, and it's the best position in the world to start your new way of thinking. You may consider yourself small in comparison to the wonders that you see, but even small things have their place and are as essential to the whole as the large things that make you feel inspired and happy. Without a grain of sand on the beach, there is no beach. Without the leaves in the forest, there are no trees.

Consider yourself as one leaf and approach life from a humbler and less judgmental stance.

You can also use mindful meditation during the course of your day by moving yourself somewhere where you can be alone and simply breathe – perhaps the corner of a park at lunchtime or on an empty sports field while at school. Allow the scents of life, the hot and cold and the sights and sounds surrounding you to be all you need to get into that moment while dismissing any thoughts, judgements or worries that may arise from your day so far or something you expect to occur later. Another method you can use is focused meditation, where you keep your eyes open but focus on something you consider inspirational or mesmerizing, such as the flicker of a candle, a vase of flowers, or a Buddha statue – something that helps you to become more aware of this moment in time. Concentrate on the focal point while you breathe and count. If you find your mind wanders, again, dismiss the thought and return to your focal point. When we are surrounded by noise and confusion, it becomes difficult to concentrate on simply being. We are too busy multitasking and trying to juggle the balancing act of our lives, and your life deserves more attention than you think.

Mindful meditation is best completed when you're calm, and the best times to take advantage of this are early in the morning before the world has started to stir, or early in the evening when the world is calming down. One easy mistake to avoid is doing this after eating or drinking. The point of meditation is to calm the mind and to prepare it for the day or the evening. The preparation of meditation brings a certain sense of wellbeing to you when you start to see things from another perspective – one that is bathed in hope and positivity. If you make this a part of your daily routine, you will start to notice changes in the way you approach life, simply because of the basic, yet effective mindfulness training you are practicing. You will remember the discussion I mentioned earlier by Neuroscientist Sara Lazar who didn't believe that mindfulness worked, however, discovered through her study that it has the power to physically alter the brain's development and function. You need to commit yourself to daily mindful practice and, when it becomes a habit, life suddenly becomes much easier to handle. Millennials, in particular, will find that life is lived in the fast lane most of the time, and effective mindfulness practices and meditation techniques will help to approach life with a sense of calm that cannot be purchased through a product or subscription that drains your pockets and leaves you in a worse place. The control gained in developing your instincts and decision-making skill is invaluable, and you will quickly discover clarity and capability in dealing with challenging situations at home and work, and personal issues that often surround these environments. Now more than ever, mindfulness can be an extremely powerful tool to introduce to your daily routine and is quickly gaining the recognition it deserves by health professional worldwide outside of a religious context.

## Chapter 6: Advanced Steps In Mindfulness

Handling Distractions

Once you have spent at least one week (more if you think that it will be beneficial), then you are ready to take it to the next step.

The next step will continue to utilize a space that deprives your physical senses of input - i.e., no sound, smell, sight, taste and tactile stimuli. Instead, you are left with your own thoughts. Many people find that their thoughts can be significant hurdles to mindfulness and they are constantly distracted by it. Don't get yourself worked up over it. You are not designed to empty your mind to the point of zero thoughts. That is not the goal of mindfulness, but you are required to refrain from participating in the thoughts that are not initiated by you.

Distractions

Distractions are not really distractions at all. Thoughts, regardless of whether they are positive or negative, are the way the mind works when it is not directed. The human body is a manifestation of energy and it is the nexus between nothing and something.

Between nothing and something!

The great pyramids of Egypt, the Great Wall of China, and the Space Shuttle. These are all great accomplishments of the human species. Each of these iconic achievements was nothing more than just a thought - a flash of energy. That flash of energy erupted from nothing, and man made that (which was nothing), into something. As man is the nexus between nothing and something.

That spark of energy that resides in a world that is not physical, residing in our minds, is a thought and that thought must not be suppressed. Instead, that thought must be channeled. These thoughts, when they are not channeled, are what we call distractions. A mind that is not at peace, or one that is not utilized well, will be prone to distractions. Removing these distractions does not mean we need to remove our thoughts, it just means we need to remove our idle mind. Amazingly enough, the cure to remove an idle mind, is mindfulness.

By being mindful, repeatedly, the idle quality of some minds before beginning the practice will gradually subside and it will sharpen the mind. As this happens, the distractions of the mind will also subside and the sessions of mindfulness will increase in intensity.

Handling Distractions

As mentioned in the last section, the way to handle natural distractions that happen in the mind, all one needs to do is constantly practice mindfulness and to do it by watching your own breath. This creates two benefits worth discussing. One is the cadence of a person's breath being a frequency that can help bring calm. The second benefit of using breath as the tool to turn on mindfulness is that breathing is always with you. Even if you were marooned naked on a lost island, the one thing you will have is your breath.

Always return to watching your breath and you will not stray far from being mindful.

The objective of the next stage of your practice is to learn how to return to your mindful state when you are distracted. This takes some practice.

As you sit in the darkness and attempt to watch your breathing, you will have thoughts, memories, and fantasies mostly random in nature, entering your conscious perception. Do not reject it, do not engage it and do not advance it. Any sort of emotion from you, be it positive or negative, will propagate the thought and expand its tentacles into associated thoughts. Soon, one small distraction will have you thinking about some mundane event from childhood.

The best way to handle these situations is to make a point of thinking about it this way before the session starts come to the realization, that your thoughts will not distract you. The first few times will be frustrating, as you will get distracted. Soon enough, your mind will learn to let it go. Keep practicing the art of pulling back from a random thought. At first, it may take a few minutes to extract yourself from one thought. It will shorten in time to minutes then to a few seconds and finally you will be able to do it at will. Each time a distraction appears, you will be able to keep your mind in the moment. Eventually, as your mind strengthens and it is no longer idle, the random thoughts will diminish considerably.

The distractions that present themselves during your attempt at being mindful will eventually be shrunk from two sides. As you strengthen your mind and learn how to be in the moment, your mind will stop the idle distractions. The second way will be the increased ability to return to mindfulness without engaging the thoughts that do infrequently come about. Handling distractions is like lifting weights - the more you practice the more you can lift.

## Chapter 7: Mindfulness And Cbt For Improving Your Mindset

By using the techniques in the last chapter, you'll find you're able to increase your wakefulness, your mood and your general performance on a regular basis.

But now we come to the next trick – changing your mood instantly and switching from one mental state to another. What we really need to be able to do in order to perform at our very best is to switch to a stressed and motivated state when something requires our attention, to become angry in a controlled manner when we're arguing and to switch off and relax from work when we get home in order to allow our brain to recover and to actually enjoy ourselves. Having an understanding of our neuroscience will help and so will having a good foundation of health. But now we're going to take full control of our mental state and our attention.

It's All About Perception

As mentioned earlier, our experiences are largely what control our emotions. Simply seeing a lion is enough to trigger a cascade of different changes in the brain that ultimately result in us becoming highly aroused both mentally and physically.

When tired, you could wake yourself by taking that cold shower or by seeing a lion! When you're drunk, it's because you have excess GABA in your brain. But if your friend gets hurt, the rush of epinephrine and dopamine will be enough to actually make you feel sober and sharp again so that you can deal with the crisis.

But what if the lion wasn't there and you only thought the lion was there?

What if the lion was there and you didn't see it?

Ultimately, it is not the actual lion that triggers the response but rather your perception of that lion and your beliefs about the lion.

Put it another way: if you were to see a lion and you didn't know what a lion was, then you probably wouldn't have the same fight or flight response – you might even think it looked cute and get an oxytocin release instead!

It's your understanding of the situation that impacts on the way you react to it and this in turn changes the way you feel and the way you behave.

And this is actually what happens all the time throughout our lives to a lesser extent. This is why some people are calm and relaxed all the time (we call them 'laid back') while other people are constantly stressed and anxious.

Let's imagine you're in your office and you have a very bad deadline that you don't think you can meet. Some of you might now feel incredibly stressed and thus experience that fight or flight response. But others among you might not have that response at all and you may instead find you're able to stay very calm and collected.

There's of course an ideal middle ground here – being too stressed is bad for your health and can actually cause you to become less productive in some cases (the response is sometimes actually referred to as the fight, flight or freeze response!) while being too relaxed as mentioned can cause you to end up not actually doing anything about the situation.

The simple fact of the matter is that in these situations, some people see a lion and some people see a cat. The scenario is the precise same but their reaction to that situation can be very different. This is based on your life experiences, diet, health and personality – but you can take control of it once you know how.

The Idea Behind CBT

CBT is 'cognitive behavioral therapy', which in turn is a type of psycho-therapeutic intervention that is based almost entirely around the concepts we've just discussed. This asserts that our behavior is a result of our associations (this is behaviorism) and of our thought processes that actually al-low us to reinforce an idea in our heads.

So when faced with a stressful situation, you will be stressed partly be-cause of the beliefs and associations you hold regarding that situation. At the same time, you'll then start playing out what you expect to happen in your head and when this happens, areas of the brain fire almost as though that thing were really happening. You might imagine getting fired, having your house repossessed, or being injured depending on the scenario.

This then causes the release of even more stress hormones, just as though you were really in those situations and you can end up anxious, aroused and potentially less effective. This is where a lot of phobias come from but it's also what can make us less self-confident, less likely to take positive risks and generally less successful than we otherwise could be.

So CBT aims to change this, partly by creating new associations and partly by changing the way you think and changing what you're visualizing.

There's more to it than that of course but this is the central concept and the tools used to this end are collectively referred to as 'cognitive restructuring'.

So let's say that you want to be calmer at work, or you want to overcome a fear of heights. How might you do that using CBT? The first step would be to become more aware of your existing thoughts, beliefs and emotions. You can do this in a number of ways. One common tool is journaling, whereby you keep a journal of your thoughts, feelings and emotions pertaining to the thing that frightens you. This way, you can really deconstruct the thought process that is leading to your fear.

Another option is to use mindfulness. This is a form of meditation that doesn't focus on making your mind blank but instead focusses on letting your mind become detached while you watch the contents of your thoughts. This process in itself is very calming and can help to prevent a fight or flight response.

Once you have the thoughts that make you stressed though – or you're aware of what you're visualizing – you can then go about deconstructing them. For example, if you're afraid of public speaking then this might mean that you picture yourself stuttering and being laughed at. If you're afraid of heights, you might think things like 'I'm going to fall'.

What you don't realize is that simply thinking these things is strengthening those neural connections and coding the experience as 'bad' and 'dangerous' making the response stronger in future.

So now you're going to unravel those beliefs and try to remove them. One way to do this is with 'thought challenging'. Thought challenging essentially means that you're going to really analyze your belief and decide if it might actually be true or not. So if you're afraid of being laughed at on stage, you're going to think about how likely people really are to laugh at you and whether or not this is something that you would do in their position. The reality? Most people are kind enough and mature enough to just politely wait for you to get it back together. If anything, they'll probably only sympathize. You can also help this process by coming up with contingency plans. In other words, if you do stutter, what can you do to make it less devastating? Probably just make a joke of it to ease tension!

Also: do you really care if these strangers who you'll never see again think any less of you?

Another scenario might be low level anxiety that you're holding about your job because you're afraid of being fired. Let's say you made a big mistake on a report that won't come to light for two weeks –

now you're worried you'll be severely reprimanded.

So let's address this situation logically with thought challenging: is your boss really that harsh and unfair? Aren't there laws that would protect you? Can't you explain that it's an honest mistake? Could you blame it on your tiredness or stress at the time? If you really did get fired, wouldn't you be able to land back on your feet? Now picture the way it's much more likely to go and let that sink in. Suddenly, it's not so scary.

In both these situations you have taken that mental lion and turned it into a small kitten! You've neutered the dragon and you can thus remain much calmer thanks to your new perception of the situation. And the more you practice this, the more you'll find you start to adopt it and it starts to be-come a part of who you are. Suddenly, you'll be able to stay calm and collected during all kinds of crises at work and eventually people will start to turn to you for advice whenever something goes wrong!

Another tool is even more powerful than this and it's called 'hypothesis testing'. The problem is, that in order for you to really be able to overcome a fear or phobia, you have to really believe what you're thinking and visualizing. It's not enough to just keep saying that it's a cat and not a lion – you have to really believe it right in your heart.

So the next logical question at this point, is how you can convince yourself of your new thoughts and beliefs. And one way to do that is to use hypothesis testing – simply proving to yourself that your old beliefs were wrong and your new ones are right.

In the case of the person afraid of public speaking, what would that mean? It would mean actually making a mistake in public on person – or even standing there not saying anything for a while. You're facing your worst case scenario, trialling the worst outcome and hopefully proving to yourself that there's actually nothing to be afraid of. In doing this, you should find that no one laughs and people just wait politely. At this point, you now know that your fears were unfounded and you will find they bother you much less in future.

This is also a little like reassociation or exposure therapy. By consistently exposing yourself to the situation you used to be afraid of, you can create new associations and remove those old negative ones. You can even eventually become desensitized as you learn that there's nothing to be afraid of. I've seen a paratrooper whose heart rate remained at 60 bpm throughout the entire jump. Why? Because he'd done it hundreds of times before and his body knew that this was nothing to be afraid of.

You can work your way up to this if you're unsure but just exposing yourself to these dangerous situations will eventually be enough to help you over-come an unwanted physiological response.

One of the most powerful and effective uses for this? Becoming socially bulletproof. Almost all of us have some kind of natural anxiety when talking to strangers and this causes us to have a minor stress response. As mentioned, this then makes us appear unconfident and sends the signal that we are the inferior party in the interaction – again, it all dates back to our evolution.

But if you keep exposing yourself to new social situations and even make them purposefully awkward, then eventually you can completely get rid of any anxiety you previously felt at all. Try going to a shop (not one near you) and ordering your items in a funny accent. You'll find they politely nod and give you your things without saying anything. Try chatting to people you don't know on the street – even picking up the phone a bit more and calling people by typing in random numbers. The more you do this, the more accustomed you'll become to speaking with strangers and the less of a stress response you'll have in future.

By the end, you'll find that you're perfectly able to speak with complete, calm confidence in almost every situation!

## Chapter 8: The Bubble Around Us

Imagine that you have an invincible bubble around you. This bubble is pressing itself on you. It is pressing itself even more on you when you are around other people. Maybe when you are around a certain person or group of people, this pressure becomes even stronger. The purpose of this bubble is to keep your energy low, to make your body feel stiff and make you self-conscious. When this bubble pressing itself on you the most, it feels like you're carrying the world on your shoulders. You maybe feel like there is a tight band around your head. Now, what if I told you that this bubble exists? Would you want to break out of it?

I bet you answered yes. This is not as difficult as it might appear, it's actually pretty simple. However, I must say that it is not easy. But if you have the right motivation, (which I guess you have if you asked yourself the questions in chapter 1) then you'll accomplish this. You will become free from this bubble and you'll experience freedom from anxiety. Similar to the ego, this bubble wants you to identify with it. It wants you to believe that the bubble is you. This could not be further from the truth. You are so much more.

So what does this mean practically speaking? Well, the emotions that you experience when you get anxiety is not a part of who you are. It's not a curse that was given to you by birth. It's not a part of your DNA that you can't get rid of. So understand that you can always become free. It comes back to making the decision to become free. Now this requires self-awareness and courage, something I get a feeling you have since you're still reading this book. Now I will warn you that you'll have to stay somewhat grounded in this process since the feeling of freedom might overwhelm you. You might have so much suppressed emotions coming out in this process. Basically, what I'm trying to say is: Don't do anything too crazy. I don't want you to hurt yourself and like I said in the introduction, you're not going to become a god even if you feel like one.

What you'll discover is the normal state. Guess what, life is meant to be lived with a feeling of joy. That's the normal state. So if you feel like you've been locked in a cave for ages and you've finally seen the light again, congratulations.

Okay, so the goal here is to break free from the bubble. I want you to get a pen and piece of paper and write this down. I'll not explain all the details to why you should write it down but to keep it short, studies have shown over and over again that writing down your goals is the most powerful way. It will program your subconscious mind to focus on accomplishing what you have written down. Write down your goals as if they have already happened. I want you to write down, at least, these two goals yourself with your own words:

1. I am finally free from the bubble and feel so grateful for it.

2. I am free from the thought and feelings of caring about what other thinks of me.

Goal number two is actually a benefit that you'll get from breaking free from the bubble, but write it down just in case your mind feels that the bubble is a little bit too unclear and sounds too much like hokus pokus. Okay so now you know where our destination with this is. In the next chapter, we'll go into the action plan for breaking free from this bubble.

Key Takeaways:

•The purpose of the bubble is to keep your energy low, to make your body feel stiff and make you self-conscious.

•The bubble that's around us is similar to the ego, it wants you to identify with it. It wants you to believe that the bubble is you. This could not be further from the truth. You are so much more.

- Life is meant to be lived with a feeling of joy. That's the normal state.
- Write down your goal, so your subconscious mind knows where to look and what direction you are going.

## Chapter 9: Basics Of Mindfulness Meditation

If there is one single word that is used a lot these days, then it has to be mindfulness. However, it is mainly used for good reason. As earlier explained, this is a simple practice that can improve both the physical and mental health, boost one's self-confidence, and assist to see you calm in situations that are stressful.

Basically, being mindful is allowing yourself to be entirely present in the current moment you are in. It is a situation where you take away all the judgments and just allow a particular moment to remain the way it is. It means that you take time to notice all the little details from sounds to colors, and then come up with a real sense of "being". Oftentimes, we opt to be still, the mind will fill with all manner of things that we need to do, the kind of things that worry us, and other things we need to do immediately after.

This is how it is – physically, we have sat there, but our minds have wandered off to another place. Now, this is where the whole issue of being mindful comes in. all it requires you to do is to take all your focus away from your thoughts and get back after some moment.

In the same manner, if we were to sit in a quiet park, our minds will be shifted to the blue shades that are on the sky, the sounds of the chirping birds, as well as the temperature of the air. Our attention, in doing so, shall have moved from the thoughts that are in our heads, to the real things that we can see, feel, and hear. It is just doing that without thinking.

There is no particular way to be mindful. You can decide to make it as simple as just listening to a friend talk or as complicated as attending to half an hour meditation. What is important is that you have taken time to be mindful, regardless of how big or small the act may be to you. The main aim of mindfulness is to help us put certain space between ourselves and the reactions that we have, and in return, breaking down the conditioned responses.

Getting Started

Here are some of the ways you can use to tune into mindfulness all through the day:

**You should set aside some time** – You actually don't need a meditation bench or cushion to achieve this, or even any type of special tool to gain access to the mindfulness skills that you got. However, it will be important for you to set aside some space and time.

**Just observe the present moment, as it is** – Remember that the main aim of mindfulness is not really quieting the mind, or even trying to achieve a state of eternal calm. There is a very simple goal here: just paying attention to the present moment, and this should be done without any kind of judgment. It is, however, easier said than done.

**Allow your judgments to roll by** – We can easily make a mental note of any form of judgment that might arise in course of our practice. The best thing we can do for them is just to let them pass.

Again, observe the present moment as it is – In most cases, our minds get carried away in thought. That is one of the reasons why mindfulness has been described as the practice of returning to the present moment, again and again, without ceasing.

**To your wandering mind, just be kind** – You should not judge yourself for any kind of thought that might pop up. All you need to do is to crop up and practice the art of recognizing when your mind has wandered off. In the end, make sure you bring it back, as it is required.

**Consider Mindful Moving** – It does not really matter the kind of action you could be involved in – running, riding your bike, or just walking, all you need to do is to think of the action. Pay great attention to your breathing, the instant your feet get into contact with the floor and the view of the nature that you are passing. You will notice that you are less lost in thought and have more of a chance to appreciate your surrounding.

**Focus more on your breathing** – If there is one of the easiest ways of becoming mindful, then it has to be placing your focus on the way you breathe. You should notice how fast you breathe in, how deep the breath is, and the manner in which your chest rises down and up. This will quickly ease the thoughts that have filled your mind, and replace them with a feeling that is way much lighter.

**Work through the senses** – Making a stop to focus on what you can see, feel, smell, and hear is very important, regardless of the moment you are in. this is one of the ways of removing judgments and just taking note of the physical aspects of the world that is around you.

**Meditation is key** – There is a difference between mindfulness and meditation. Meditation is more centered on creating awareness to yourself, while mindfulness usually includes the main focus on what is around you. Having said that, mindfulness is, therefore, a type of meditation that can only be mastered by meditating.

**Mindful eating is also important** – Most times we are eating, we try to do a number of other things all at once. They might include sending a text message to a friend, or even scrolling via social media. Each time we do this, we do not feel as nourished and satisfied by taking the meals. You should take time to eat slowly, and focus on the taste of the food. There is a special time that comes with eating – you should enjoy it.

**Listen with intent** – Each time we are having a conversation, we naturally spend the time that a person is talking to us thinking about the kind of reply we should give. What this means is that we are not actually listening to what they should say. Being a mindful listener means that you have to focus on what a person is saying, the emotions you are able to sense, as well as their body language.

Even though it might appear so simple, there are several benefits that come with being mindful.

First of all, it creates increased gratitude. Each time we are mindful, we get appreciative. We will spend less time focusing on what we do not have and even create time to be thankful for the little things that we have in life, which might include a scent that reminds of the past memories, or a bright blue sky.

It also gives us a clearer mind. Essentially, mindfulness is all about appreciating a particular situation without judgment, and that would allow you to be more open-minded. In the end, you will be able to find peace in a situation that could have been filled with unending worry.

The practice of mindfulness also encourages positivity. Far from many people believe, mindfulness does not really try to get rid of the negative thoughts. However, it tends to offer several ways of thinking around the negative thoughts by offering you a moment where all your struggles are not the whole focus of your mind.

Finally, the practice also relaxes physically, since it basically involves focusing the mind. Each time we feel stressed, it will manifest in our bodies, and that will lead to uncomfortable and tensed situations. Encouraging space in the mind, where there is less stress, will train your body to naturally relax.

Developing Mindfulness Meditation

One thing that has become clear throughout this eBook is that cultivating mindfulness is the key to recognizing natural wisdom and overcoming suffering; both for us and for others. In the Buddhist tradition and the training of contemplative psychotherapy, mindfulness is nurtured through the practice of sitting meditation.

There are many forms of meditation, but most of them are designed to just make us relax, and create altered states of consciousness. What makes mindfulness meditation unique is the fact that it is not directed towards having us to be different from the way we already are. But instead, it assists us in becoming aware of facts, which are already true each moment.

It would be right to say it trains us on becoming unconditionally present; as in, it helps us to be present with what is going on at a particular moment, regardless of what it is. You could wonder what importance that has. After all, we just need to suffer less. And, aren't we interested in adopting this brilliant sanity, and natural wisdom that we have been told about? Will they change anything from we already have?

The answer to these questions could be either yes or no. First of all, being more conversant with our inbuilt weaknesses and suffering less would be changes from the manner in which we experience ourselves at the moment, or maybe most of the time. Secondly, the way to alleviate suffering and uncover the brilliant sanity is through going more deeply into the present moment and also into ourselves in the manner we are, and not to try to alter what is already going on.

The sitting practice of mindfulness meditation offers us this exact opportunity to be more present with ourselves just the way we are. In return, this will show us a glimpse of the inherent wisdom and also teaches us how to stop perpetuating the unnecessary suffering that comes as a result of trying to run away from the life's discomfort, and even pain that we experience inevitably as a consequence for just being alive. It has also been shown in the previous chapters that Buddha taught us that the primary source of suffering is our unplanned attempt to run away from the direct experiences that we encounter.

The first consequence of this is that we cause ourselves suffering by attempting to run away from pain and trying unsuccessfully to hang on to short-lived pleasure. But as unfortunate as it may appear, this strategy does not perpetuate our happiness or quell our suffering, but has the opposite effect. As opposed to making us happy, it will pose us to more suffering. The second consequence of this comes when we attempt to prop up a false identity, always known as ego. This also does not work, and will lead us to unnecessary suffering.

While paying nonjudgmental attention to our experiences as they subsides and arises, mindfulness does not reject anything. Instead of working so hard to break loose from the experiences that we find to be complicated, we end up practicing how to cope up with them. We also introduce mindfulness to pleasant experiences as well. Surprisingly though, many times we experience hard times when it comes to staying just present with the happiness we have attained so far. We end up turning it into something that sounds more familiar, such as worrying that it will not last or even trying to keep it from disappearing.

Each time we become mindful, we will show up for our lives and don't wish things to be different or being distracted by some other events. But when there is something that should be changed, we become present enough to understand all that should be done. That is one of the basics of mindfulness meditation. As a matter of fact, being mindful cannot be described as a substitute for really being present in our daily lives and taking care of our lives and that of others. The more mindful we get, the more skillful we will be in the compassionate action.

So, the question that comes up again is how we can practice mindfulness meditation. Again, it is important to note that there are various basic techniques involved here. If your interest is in pursuing mindfulness within a given tradition such as the Buddhist ones or any other, then it might be important to get in touch with a meditation instructor.

There are 3 basic aspects that are worked within a meditation technique: They include the following;

- Body
- Breath
- Thoughts

First of all, we relate to the body, which includes the manner in which we set up the environment. Due to the fact that we usually apply meditation in preparing to work with other people around us, we use a practice that is called eyes-open. That will make what we have in front of us the main factor in our practice. There are really very few people who can dedicate an entire room to their practice of meditation – setting aside a spot or a corner of a room in their home where they can easily set up a quiet space for meditating.

If you prefer, you can opt to make a small altar of some sort and decorate it with sacred objects, and pictures from your own tradition. You might also need to light candles and burn incense to remind you of the impermanence that these represent, but can still meditate with just a plain wall in front of you. As long as you are not sitting in front of something that could be distracting such as your computer desk or a TV set, it does not really matter what could be in front of you.

Once you have taken up a spot, it will be important to choose the kind of seat you will use. It is okay to sit either on a chair or on a cushion placed on the floor. If your choice is a cushion, then you can use the ones designed for meditation practice such as gomden or zafu. You can also opt to use a folded up blanket or some other sort of low bench. The key point here is to have a seat that will not wiggle you around or is unstable.

If your choice is to sit on a chair, then you should pick one that has a flat seat and does not tilt too much going to the back. For those who are short, it would be important to place something on the floor for your feet to rest on, which will take some little weight. You don't need something that will make your legs dangling in an uncomfortable manner. For those who have long legs, and are generally tall, the key is to make the hips higher than the knees, either on a cushion or a chair. Failure to do that will cause backaches pretty fast.

Once you have your spot and your seat, you should just go ahead and have a seat. You should take a posture that is not rigid, but upright. The main idea here is to adopt a posture that will reflect your inherent good sanity, one that wont be stiff, but delightful. The back is always straight with the lower back curve that would naturally be there. Think of this – for a moment, imagine that your spine was a tree and lean against it. Maybe that might work for you, give it a try.

While sitting on a cushion, just cross your legs comfortably in front of you. There is no absolute need to contort yourself in postures that are not comfortable. All you can do is to just cross your legs, the way you might have done as a kid. Again, you should not forget that your hips should be higher than your knees.

If possible, you should think of adding more height to your seat by holding up a towel or a blanket.

The hands should rest on the thighs as they face down. The eyes should be open, and the gaze should rest gently on the floor in front of you nearly 6 feet away. If you are seating close to the wall than that, then you should let your gaze rest on the wall each time it lands. The gaze should not be tightly focused. The main idea is that what is in front of you is what is in front of you. Do not do anything special or stare with the gaze, but just allow it to rest at the place you have set it.

Let your back be strong, and your front be open

Start by just sitting in this kind of posture for a few minutes. If you realize that your attention is wandering away, then gently bring it back to the environment and your body. Your mind will definitely wonder, since it is part of mindfulness – minds have to wander. However, you should find a way of bringing it back gently.

Working with the breath is the second part of the practice. In this particular practice, you should lightly rest your attention on the breath to achieve all you have been looking for.

You should feel it as if it is coming into your body and it is moving out. There is no particular way of breathing in this type of methodology. Note that you should only be interested in how you already are, and not the way you are if you manipulate your breath. If along the way, you notice that you are controlling your breath in a certain way, then you should just let it be that way. It is not easy to be natural on purpose, it will not easily work. Therefore, you shouldn't get caught in worrying about whether your breath is natural or not. You should just let it be the way it.

Take time again to sit for a few minutes in harmony with your breath, environment and posture. Breathing in and out is, at times, quantified as 25% of the attention you have on your breath. The main point here is not to score everything right, but to offer you an idea that you are not directing all your attention tightly on the breathing patterns. The rest of your attention will be on the environment and your breath.

The last part of this technique would be on how to work with thoughts. As you go on with your practicing session, you will realize that several thoughts arise. At times, the thoughts could be several, even overlapping one over the other including fantasies, future plans, memories, and even some bits taken from TV adverts. There may appear to be no loopholes at all in which you are able to catch a glimpse of the way you breathe. This is normal, particularly if you are doing meditation for the first time. Just sit there and take note of the actions as they unfold.

When you finally come to the realization that you are so much caught in thoughts that you even forget that you are sitting in a room, just find a way of bringing yourself back to the breath. As a further reminder of what has just taken place, you can mentally say "thinking" to yourself. This kind of labeling is not entirely a judgment, but rather a neutral observation.

In summary, you shouldn't forget that mindfulness meditation is all about practicing on being mindfulness regardless of what might happen. It is not a process where we get ourselves to stop thinking. It is so easy to fall into the trap of believing that the goal of this is to stop us from thinking. There are those who have mistaken the idea that becoming blank is the main aim of mindfulness meditation. It could be in certain other approaches, but not in mindfulness meditation.

So, if you find yourself deeply buried in thinking, you should not dismiss the thoughts. All we are trying to do, through mindfulness meditation, is to be ourselves as we already are, and not trying hard to convert ourselves into a kind of preconceived ideas of how we should instead be.

## Chapter 10: Why People Find Mindfullness At Work Advantageous

Why People Find Mindfullness at Work Advantageous

Take out any of the well-reputed brands such as Google, NHS, and Transport; you would see the managers suggest their employees keep up mindfulness at work. But what is this mindfulness? Why this is so significant for their employees! Let me tell you; mindfulness is nothing but the awareness-awareness to the present condition without any doubt. And it is nothing new; rather people used to practice it since the time of Buddhism. Yes, that's true; later people start to apply it for their purpose regardless of any religion, culture and other distinctions.

Why is mindfulness necessary?

All of the concerned studies about it conclude that it is very significant to reduce stress, conflict, and anxiety. On the other hand, it would increase resilience and emotional intelligence to a great extent among the people. All of these would improve the communication level of the employees as well.

When would you need it?

Although it is benign to all the people working throughout the day; you definitely need help from a professional mindfulness at work service in the following conditions:

• If you have grown a tendency to miss out recollecting words in conversations.

•If you start forgetting your daily commute.

•Paying more attention to some electronic gadgets other than near and dear ones.

•Living in the past and cannot pay attention to the present.

If you are experiencing any of such conditions or all of such conditions then you must get help from this service.

How is it beneficial for employees!

In the current scenario, managers often encourage employees to take more work pressure, doing works for hours after hours. As a result; the employees soon become psychologically deactivated; their personal lives get hampered, their dedication level gets hurt. And so, the company would suffer loss instead of make some impressive profits. Now, look at how this service can prove to be advantageous to all of them.

• A proper mindfulness at work program would elevate those professionals by offering neurological benefits

• Now, betters psychological calmness would lead to better communication level as well.

• It will also help you to make alternative strategies to accomplish a hard task.

• In short, your brain would start controlling your emotion, desire and so on.

To make a long story short, this kind of service has more psychological benefits rather than physical benefits. That's why managers apply this in their workplace for their employees and thus they ensure better productivity from them.

## Chapter 11: Boosting Resilience

The fact is that we are going to encounter difficulties no matter where we go. Some of us will be quick to throw in the towel at the slightest difficulty, whereas others will seem to thrive on challenges. The people who are unbowed by life's challenges, those who fight back tirelessly are the ones who ultimately live their dreams. The rest — the weaklings — are quickly buried in the heavy pages of life. Challenges will always be there. But it is upon us to decide whether we will take on our challenges or give in. Standing on your two feet and fighting back is no joke. But the good thing is that anyone can develop resilience as long as they are committed. Mindfulness is a major mental training that enhances our capacity to be resilient and fight back against life's difficulties. The following are some of the ways that mindfulness promotes resilience.

Flexible

Everyone is stuck in a situation that is only unique to them. When we encounter a problem, our kneejerk reaction is to apply the tactics that worked elsewhere in the hopes of a similar outcome. But we fail to realize that these are entirely different situations. Through mindfulness, we learn the value of being flexible and adjusting to the demands of life and testing out various methods until we come to the one that works.

Taking our lessons

We must always understand that there's life beyond the challenges that we go through. It doesn't matter the nature of the challenge. It will pass. But these challenges should enlighten us, make us wiser. In the future, there might be a repeat of the same, but we should be in a position to remedy the problem.

Relationships

We never quite recognize the importance of having connections, having people on your side, until we are faced with life difficulties. It is during those challenging times that we look around for help. Mindfulness allows us to develop close ties with people so that we may help one another in times of distress.

Release tension

When our minds are consumed with thoughts of constant fights, the tension can easily build up inside of us. But we have to learn to let go of this tension so that we can have the energy to keep charting. Mindfulness equips with the tools of getting rid of the pent up emotions and energy and turning on a new leaf.

Cultivate healthy habits

Mindfulness empowers you to develop the best habits when you go through a rough patch. Let's say that your business is on the verge of collapsing because of impending bankruptcy. The financial institutions are after your neck and you are obviously shaken. You are at risk of diving into negative habits like overeating, sex addiction, and alcoholism. But thanks to mindfulness, you are driven into positive habits instead and you may start exercising, meditating, and reading your favorite genre.

Believing in yourself

Unless you strongly believe in yourself, chances are you will want to throw in the towel and run off to hide. But such an action would have your enemies in celebration mood. No matter how bleak the situation looks, you have got to be resilient. Mindfulness empowers you to believe in yourself and this is precisely what makes you stay in the fight until you win.

Sense of humor

Mindfulness allows you to see the fun side to your troubles. This attitude has certainly helped men overcome their troubles and live to the fullest. For instance, during the world wars, many commanders were reputed to have a sense of humor and even though they had been living in constant fear for their lives, knowing that one foot wrongly placed would bring about their end in an explosion, they would take their time to appreciate a good joke.

Positivity

Unless you are operating from an angle of positivity, you will always be at the mercy of your opponents. But when you are positive that you will emerge triumphantly, no challenge is too great for you. Regular practice of mindfulness bestows the aura of positivity around us so that we have the courage to face off our challenges.

Helping others

By stopping to help others, we are doing ourselves a tremendous favor. Acts of altruism make us feel worthy and improve our fighting spirit. So, when we reach out to other people who are hurting, we increase the resolve to overcome our challenges.

Embrace new perspectives

It has been shown time and again that taking on a new perspective will change the whole scenario. When we are up against a challenge, the last thing on our minds is changing our perspective. We want to take a solid stance. But in some instances, having a fresh perspective might make us see the challenge in an entirely new fashion – perhaps not as a challenge anymore, but as something to be embraced. There are various mindfulness techniques that are aimed at flexing our cognitive muscles so that we may approach challenges from different perspectives. We can also acquire new perspectives through habits that expand our imagination, for instance, reading books and researching.

Acceptance

It is through accepting our circumstances for what they are that we become inspired to take action. Being afraid of facing our reality holds us back. Most people have a tendency of throwing blame around in difficult times. This indicates a lack of acceptance. Mindfulness teaches us how to be accepting of our reality and make decisions that are going to turn our lives for the better. Before you develop a streak of resilience, you first have to accept that you are in a vulnerable position and work on improving your condition.

## Chapter 12: How To Manage Thoughts To Control Anxiety

Anxiety can cause physical indications like a quick heartbeat and sweat-soaked hands. It can make you limit your exercises and can make it difficult to make an amazing most.

Healthy thinking can enable you to forestall or control uneasiness.

•Negative thoughts can expand your stress or dread.

•CBT, is a sort of treatment that can assist you supplant negative considerations with precise, empowering ones.

•Changing your thinking will take some time. You have to rehearse sound reasoning each day. Sooner or later, solid reasoning will work out easily for you.

•Healthy thinking may not be sufficient to help a few people who have stress and uneasiness. Call your primary mindfulness physician or advisor if you think you need more help.

How might you utilize healthy thinking to adapt to anxiety?

Notice and stop your thoughts

The initial step is to notice and stop your negative thoughts or "self-talk." Self-talk is the thing that you ponder yourself and your encounters. It resembles a running editorial in your mind. Your self-talk might be objective and accommodating. Or on the other hand it might be negative and not supportive.

Get some information about your considerations

The following stage is to ask yourself whether your musings are useful or unhelpful. See what you're stating to yourself. Does the proof help your negative idea? A portion of your self-talk might be valid. Or on the other hand it might be halfway evident however misrepresented.

Perhaps the most ideal approaches to check whether you are stressing an excessive amount of is to take a gander at the chances. What are the chances, or possibilities, that the awful thing you are stressed over will occur? If you have a vocation audit that has one little analysis among numerous compliments, what are the chances that you truly are in risk of losing your employment? The chances are likely low.

There are a few sorts of unreasonable contemplations. Here are a couple of types to search for:

•**Focusing on the negative:** This is some of the time called sifting. You channel out the great and spotlight just on the terrible. Model: "I get so apprehensive talking openly. I simply realize that individuals are considering how terrible I am at speaking." Reality: Probably nobody is more centered around your exhibition than you. It might search for some proof that beneficial things occurred after one of your introductions. Did individuals hail a short time later? Did anybody reveal to you that you worked admirably?

•**Should:** People once in a while have set thoughts regarding how they "should" act. On the off chance that you hear yourself saying that you or other individuals "should," "should," or "need to" accomplish something, at that point you may set yourself up to feel terrible. Model: "I must be in charge constantly or I can't adapt to things." Reality: There's nothing amiss with needing to have some authority over the things that you can control. In any case, you may cause yourself nervousness by agonizing over things that you can't control.

•**Overgeneralizing:** This is taking one model and saying it's valid for everything. Search for words, for example, "never" and "consistently." Example: "I'll never feel typical. I stress over everything constantly." Reality: You may stress over numerous things. Be that as it may, everything? Is it conceivable you are misrepresenting? In spite of the fact that you may stress over numerous things, you likewise may find that you feel solid and quiet about different things.

**•All-or-nothing thinking:** This is additionally called dark or-white reasoning. Model: "On the off chance that I don't find an ideal line of work audit, at that point I'll lose my employment." Reality: Most execution surveys incorporate some useful analysis—something you can chip away at to improve. On the off chance that you get five positive remarks and one useful proposal, that is a decent survey. It doesn't imply that you're in risk of losing your employment.

**•Catastrophic thinking:** This is accepting that the most exceedingly terrible will occur. This kind of unreasonable reasoning regularly incorporates "imagine a scenario where" questions. Model: "I've been having cerebral pains of late. I'm so stressed. Consider the possibility that it's a brain tumor?" Reality: If you have loads of migraines, you should see a specialist. However, the chances are that it's something progressively normal and far less genuine. You may need glasses. You could have a sinus contamination. Possibly you're getting strain cerebral pains from pressure.

Choose your thoughts

The following stage is to choose an accommodating idea to supplant the unhelpful one.

Keeping a diary of your contemplations is probably the most ideal approaches to work on halting, asking, and picking your musings. It makes you mindful of your self-talk. Record any negative or unhelpful considerations you had during the day. On the off chance that you figure you probably won't recall them toward the finish of your day, keep a scratch pad with you so you can record any considerations as they occur. At that point record accommodating messages to address the negative musings.

If you do this consistently, precise, supportive contemplations will before long work out easily for you.

However, there might be a trace of validity in a portion of your negative musings. You may have a few things you need to deal with. On the off chance that you didn't execute just as you might want on something, record that. You can take a shot at an arrangement to address or improve that zone.

Ways to Calm Your Anxious Mind

Anxious thoughts can overpower you, settling on it hard to settle on choices and make a move to manage whatever issue troubles you. Anxiety can likewise prompt overthinking, which makes you increasingly restless, which prompts more overthinking, etc. How might you escape this endless loop? Subduing on edge considerations won't work; they will simply spring up once more, now and then with greater power. However, there are progressively viable procedures you can acquire from mindfulness-based pressure decrease and CBT.

Coming up next are 9 methods to enable you to get unstuck and push ahead:

**1.** Attempt Cognitive Distancing

Attempt to consider your to be contemplations as conjectures, not as certainties. Your mind is attempting to secure you by foreseeing what could occur—however in light of the fact that something could happen doesn't mean it will. See target proof: How likely is it that the negative result will really occur? Is there anything great that may occur? What's more, which do you believe is well on the way to occur, in light of past involvement and other data you have about the circumstance?

**2.** Attempt Cognitive De-Fusion

Quit being intertwined with your contemplations. Think about your musings as moving information going through your brain, as opposed to the target truth about a circumstance. Our brains are extremely touchy to risk and threat since this kept our predecessors alive in nature. A portion of your contemplations may simply be programmed molded responses created by a mind that is situated to endurance. Pick whether to accept these contemplations, as opposed to simply tolerating them.

**3.** Practice Mindfulness

Work on watching your musings, as opposed to responding consequently to them. Think about your musings as mists gliding by. Which attract you and which make you need to flee? Is there a way you can unwind yourself and simply watch your musings, as opposed to responding?

**4.** Concentrate on Direct Experience

Your mind makes up anecdotes about what your identity is, and about your wellbeing and adorableness. Not these accounts are exact. Now and again our minds are one-sided by negative past encounters. What is your involvement right now? Is this something that is really occurring or something that may occur? Notice that they are not something very similar, despite the fact that your brain may regard them as the equivalent.

**5.** Label Things

Label the sort of thought you are having, as opposed to focusing on its substance. Watch your musings and when you see a judgment (e.g., how fortunate or unfortunate the circumstance is), feel free to mark it as Judging. On the off chance that you see a stress (e.g., that you will fizzle or experience a misfortune) mark it as Worrying. If you are scrutinizing yourself, name it as Criticizing. This gets you away from the exacting substance of your contemplations and gives you more consciousness of your psychological procedures. Would you like to invest your energy judging and stressing? Are there less judgmental or stressed approaches to see the circumstance?

**6.** Stay in the Present

Is your mind disgorging the past? Because something negative occurred in the past doesn't mean it needs to happen today. Inquire as to whether the conditions, or your insight and adapting capacities, have changed since the last time. As a grown-up, you have progressively decision about whom to connect with and greater capacity to recognize, acquire, or leave an awful circumstance than when you were a youngster or adolescent.

**7.** Widen Your View

It is safe to say that you are concentrating too barely on the compromising parts of a circumstance, as opposed to seeing the entire picture? Uneasiness makes our brains agreement and spotlight on the quick danger without thinking about the more extensive setting. Is this circumstance truly as significant as your uneasiness says it seems to be? Will despite everything you mindfulness about this issue in 5 or 10 years? On the off chance that not, at that point simplicity up on the stress.

**8.** Get Up and Get Going

Stressing over an issue without making an answer won't enable you to take mindfulness of the issue. It might in certainty make you less inclined to act by sustaining your uneasiness. At the point when your mind is stuck in a circle, you can interfere with it by getting up and moving around or doing an alternate assignment or movement. At the point when you sit down, you ought to have an alternate point of view.

**9.** Decide Whether a Thought Is Helpful

Because an idea is genuine doesn't imply that it is useful to concentrate on—at any rate not constantly. On the off chance that lone 1 out of 10 individuals will land the position you look for, and you continue considering those chances, you may move toward becoming demotivated and not by any means try applying. This is a case of an idea that is valid however not supportive.

Concentrate on what is useful and released the rest!

## How to Manage your Activities to Reduce Anxiety

I had an "ah ha" minute a year ago that has completely changed me. Or possibly the discernment I have of my life.

Like such a significant number of individuals, I was occupied, occupied, occupied. I was shuffling heaps of balls noticeable all around without a moment's delay... two small kids, a business, a house to oversee, charitable effort to do, also tennis, my Bunco gathering and Book Club, without any end in sight. I would begin the day running and regularly fall in bed after 12 PM with just 50% of my plan for the day confirmed. "One week from now things will settle down" I'd let myself know, just to find that one week from now was similarly as occupied. I was continually anticipating when things would back off - yet that time never showed up.

Sound natural? I wager it does in light of the fact that I infrequently meet individuals who aren't pushed and overpowered attempting to complete everything.

We live in a harried, depleted society. Furthermore, I had fallen prey to the conviction that occupied is great - it implies I am beneficial, and NOT lethargic. I've even ended up boasting (camouflaged as whimpering) about the fact that I was so occupied to other people. Once in a while, I'd get into a benevolent challenge with somebody to see who was the "busiest." Now, that is crazy!

We don't get decorations for destroying ourselves - we simply get depleted!

At that point, it hit me one day. My life is occupied - however more significantly it is FULL. I am accomplishing such a significant number of things that I need to do in light of the fact that they make me glad and they fit my vision. Rather than saying, "I have a truly bustling week "- I began supplanting "occupied" with "full" - and all of a sudden, my viewpoint changed. I have an "entire week." I have a "full life". Brimming with exercises that help my family, give me reason, empower me, and are charming.

That may appear to be an extremely little and basic activity. Yet, changing that single word likewise changed my point of view - and that is POWERFUL! I started to settle on a cognizant decision to perceive the magnificence in my life. I perceived that I was so blessed to have such a significant number of chances, connections, and encounters. I remembered I would prefer not to lounge around staring at the TV and eating bon bons (in any event, not more often than not). I need a full life - brimming with joy, love and fulfillment.

I understood that everything in my life is a decision. I pick the individuals and the exercises that fill my days. Subsequently, it us up to me to settle on savvy decisions and be certain I am picking things that are satisfying and not only things to make me occupied.

At that point, I began looking nearer and when something came up that didn't feel better - that didn't feel "full" to me - I chose I expected to release that thing. Gradually, I began saying "no" to the things that weren't satisfying. Presently, when I start to feel worried by my calendar, I recognize that I am so fortunate to accomplish such a significant number of things that I cherish

Anxiety can influence your body, mind and conduct. Here are some useful tips* for overseeing anxiety by tending to these three territories.

I propose you choose a couple to begin with that appear to be most pertinent to you.

Healthy body

Physical manifestations of anxiety can incorporate muscle strain, dashing heart, dazedness, perspiring, and brevity of breath. These can happen out of the blue and be very upsetting. They can be anticipated or decreased by customary self-mindfulness and unwinding.

**1:** Nurture Yourself

Eat standard well-adjusted dinners (for example three nutritious suppers daily).

Avoid or lessen liquor, nicotine, and caffeine admission.

Exercise routinely, especially with a cardiovascular or unwinding part.

Perform customary self-mindfulness -, for example, loosening up exercises and normal arranged breaks.

Have a decent rest schedule.

2: **Breathe**

Breathing admirably can back off or interfere with the uneasiness reaction, and give a feeling of quiet, establishing, or unwinding.

Practice cognizant profound relaxing for 1 moment at once, at whatever point you are hanging tight for something (for example holding up in line, for a test to begin, when halted at a traffic light).

Try protracting your exhalation or outward breath - take in for 4 seconds and inhale out for 5 or 6 seconds. Practice this cycle a couple of minutes every day, or at whatever point you consider it.

**3:** Be Mindful

Monitoring our body and surroundings in a non-judgmental way can lessen sentiments of nervousness and bring a condition of quiet.

Close your eyes and watch your breathing: see your body, how the admission of air feels and what sensations you watch.

Shift your attention to what you can hear, smell, and contact, monitoring nature outside your body.

Shift mindfulness to and fro from your body to your surroundings a few times.

**4:** Use Cues to Relax

At the point when you know that your body is tense or you feel that you can't relinquish stress or stress, utilize this as a prompt to rehearse increasingly standard unwinding.

Try fixing and discharging diverse muscle gatherings, to work on loosening up the ones that are generally tense.

Imagine when you inhale out that any strain in your body is streaming outward, and as you take in, envision it is being supplanted by warmth, vitality, and harmony.

Think of a picture or scene that is unwinding to you, and picture this when feeling tense or under pressure.

Schedule normal unwinding and charming exercises -, for example, rub, steaming showers, work out, or being in nature.

Healthy mind

Anxiety can be joined by mental action that is upsetting, diverting and inefficient. This incorporates stress and distraction with fears or envisioned negative results. The more you stress, the more it is probably going to happen.

**5:** Be Realistic

Regularly when individuals are restless, they think about the most noticeably awful conceivable result to their circumstance, regardless of whether this is probably not going to happen. This builds nervousness and its belongings.

Notice if you are pondering your indications or circumstance.

Remind yourself that emotions are not actualities - in light of the fact that you fear a specific result, doesn't make it bound to happen or make your stresses work out.

Employ rationale - challenge yourself to think about a result or end that is not so much cataclysmic, but rather more liable to happen as a general rule. You may need to request that others help in the beginning. Record your reaction as a future update.

Think of times in the past when your stresses have refuted.

**6:** Interrupt Anxious Thinking

Now and again it's difficult to utilize coherent reasoning, particularly when uneasiness is high. Brief disturbance of on edge musings can enable you to get to your rationale and pick what you would like to concentrate on.

Identify if perpetual and capricious stress for sure 'if?' believing is an issue for you.

Try some extraordinary (and senseless) approaches to interfere with this negative procedure, for example,

Sing your stresses to a senseless tune, or talk them in an entertaining animation voice.

Pick a charming idea to concentrate on or envision, for example, something you anticipate or are pleased with doing.

Listen to music or a book recording.

Intentionally return your consideration regarding the assignment you are performing, advising yourself that stress is unhelpful.

**7:** Contain Your Worry

If your stress is difficult to control, diverts you from your day by day undertakings, and expends your reasoning, attempt a few different ways to restrict the stress and permit yourself a break.

Identify if your stress is reasonable (includes an angle inside your control) or unsolvable (outside of your control).

Use critical thinking to concentrate on reasonable stresses. Unmistakably distinguish the issue, conceptualize potential arrangements, use experts and con leans to choose the best solution(s), and make an activity arrangement to address the issue.

For unsolvable stresses, use unwinding and different methods to lessen your negative response to the circumstance.

Worry well and just once - utilize a stress diary or journal to list your stresses once per day (up to 20mins). When and if those stresses re-happen during the day, advise yourself that you have just stressed over that today.

Imagine a vacant compartment to store your stresses - envision yourself setting your stresses into this, naming them as you go, at that point rationally put on the top. Welcome a quiet idea or re-center onto the assignment you are dealing with.

**8:** Coach Yourself to Approach Situations

Some nervousness is ordinary throughout everyday life, except maintaining a strategic distance from things in regular day to day existence that we dread just makes uneasiness more grounded. On the off chance that we can approach esteemed yet anxiety inciting circumstances, they become simpler after some time and with training.

Assess your shirking - know about spots and circumstances you maintain a strategic distance from because of uneasiness however which you might want to approach.

Rate your dread of these on a 1 to 10 scale (with 1 being low degrees of anxiety and 10 being the most noteworthy conceivable uneasiness). The objective of instructing is to diminish this dread.

Assess your self-talk - What unhelpful things would you say you are educating yourself concerning the circumstance which increment anxiety?

List your objectives - How is shirking meddling with these? Record what you might want to do if anxiety was not in the manner.

Begin to rehearse in little portions enduring some anxiety without attempting to escape it promptly (you may require some assistance with this if your levels are high).

Practice instructing yourself in increasingly helpful articulations to counter negative self-talk for example 'I may feel on edge yet I am as yet ready to do this.' Think of events when you have adapted well or when the dreaded result has not happened. Record them to help remind you.

Healthy behavior

In conquering anxiety, it is generally insufficient to change our considerations alone. Improving the way, we oversee pressure and approach nervousness inciting circumstances can frequently be the most significant advance.

**9:** Reduce Over-Activity

A few people accomplish more when on edge. While high movement can lessen anxiety for the time being, as you may accomplish a few objectives, it can compound nervousness in the long haul as you feel over-worked and overpowered.

Check if over-movement is an issue for you:

Do you want to be continually occupied?

Do you think that it's difficult to back off or unwind and get increasingly on edge when you have spontaneous spare time?

Make a rundown of thoughts for back-up exercises during surprising available time, ideally a scope of unwinding or pleasant exercises (for example go to the craftsmanship exhibition, read a book) with a scope of terms. During an unforeseen extra time, pick one from your rundown.

Do not do assignments that are not your duty. Some of the time, enable others to add to assignments or help you, regardless of whether you accept they won't do it the manner in which you would.

Practice doing little undertakings incompletely (for example purposefully miss a spot when clearing the floor, or forget about a full-stop in an article). This will feel awkward, yet will enable you to loosen up additional by diminishing your emphasis on pointless subtleties.

Balance your time - Use a journal, calendar, or pie-graph to follow how you are investing energy in various territories. Ensure the classes that are essential to you are incorporated for example rest, eating, work out, social/connections, work, study, etc.

Laugh and have a fabulous time - a progressive thought, however work on giggling from your paunch. Have close by certain things that make you snicker (for example interesting pictures, messages) for use on distressing days.

**10:** Make a Plan and Practice

To feel certain and skilled utilizing the procedures you have picked, make an arrangement to rehearse these normally so they can turn out to be new, sound propensities.

Learn about uneasiness. It will lessen if you can unlearn the dread through great adapting encounters.

Become well-polished at fast quieting strategies, for example, profound relaxing for use when on edge.

Set important objectives for your life and recognize the aptitudes you have to accomplish these. Discover where/how you can get familiar with these abilities, and expand on them through training. Get help with this on the off chance that it appears to be overwhelming. Start with one little advance (the least terrifying) to approach your objective, and practice this until you feel prepared to attempt the following level.

Remember that nothing is immaculate - mishaps will happen and this is ordinary. Consider what you could realize and do any other way later on. Alter your arrangement if necessary.

## Chapter 13: Obstacles To Mindfulness And How To Get Over Them

Practicing mindfulness might seem like an easy thing to accomplish but it is actually not that simple as it seems. One of the biggest obstacles that you will have to overcome is the temptation to give up. There are a lot of people who try mindfulness for a short period of time and they give it up, the moment they notice they were not able to succeed. Instead of giving up, it might be for the best that you learn how to focus on the present. Soon, you will have found your peace of mind and you will know that you have understood mindfulness for what it actually is.

Obstacles can come in many forms and most often they appear disguised in different distractions. Your journey into the world of mindfulness will be filled with such challenges and you might have the sensation that the universe is playing with you. The distractions that can stop you from achieving peace of mind might include various problems, related to your relationship or to negative beliefs you have held on from the past. The solution is to see things as a challenge and not an obstacle. You have to take these distractions and use them in order to become more aware of the present. The more you achieve to do that, the better chances you have of discovering your true self. Each one of these distractions represents a lesson in itself, helping you grow and achieve peace of mind.

If you want to achieve peace of mind through mindfulness, don't expect for the progress to come over night. You might feel like you are progressing with the speed of a turtle, but you have to be patient and wait for the good part. In achieving such objectives, you have to let go of the attachment you have formed to different things; it will help to you concentrate more on the present and remained focused, no matter what. If you think about it, it is logic: you cannot be aware of what happens in the present, if you are constantly pondering over what happened in the past or what is going to occur in the future. By letting go of these attachments, you will find yourself being more grateful for the present. The detachment from the past will allow you to enjoy a natural progress towards the desired peace of mind.

Each journey comes with its own set of obstacles and you will have the desire to give up from time to time. When such things happen, you must remember that the hardest times are the ones that lead to the most amazing discoveries. Perception is highly important when it comes to such matters; if you know how to look at things from the right perspective, then it will be quite easy to understand that any challenge leads to peace of mind and an amazing state of relaxation.

There are a lot of people who set out clear goals when starting their journey towards mindfulness. While it is alright to have a plan and a set of objectives to reach, you must not form a strong attachment to those goals. Otherwise, you will risk those goals standing in your way of achieving the desired peace of mind. The attachment to goals that you have yet to reach will only make you feel frustrated and angry; in the end, you will end up suffering from all the negative emotions. As it was already mentioned above, detachment will allow you think clearly and achieve the goals you have set for yourself, without even knowing. If you concentrate on the present, you will find the strength and the willpower to feel relaxed and at peace with yourself.

Never forget that you are not racing towards the finish line. The journey to mindfulness is actually the destination, no matter how absurd this may sound. The rewards are found on the way and not at the finish, so you might as well take your time in taking this journey. You can set up different milestones to reach, so that you have a small sense of accomplishment but once again, do not form extreme attachments to such matters. Do not be a goal seeker but rather try to feel fulfilled and enjoy yourself on the way. The journey is the one that will help you grow and develop, the one that will make you feel better and discover peace of mind. Mindfulness is not about crossing the finishing line, it is about the journey that you take to get there. Remember that and focus on the present; the rest will work out from there.

The battle with negative emotions and attachments from the past is not an easy one to conquer. You have to learn how to deal with these thoughts and accept them without judgment, concentrating on the present and the things that are good. Accept things for what they really are and do not dwell on placing labels. Once you achieve such objectives, you will feel more at peace with yourself, discovering your inner self.

## Chapter 14: Different Types Of Meditation

There are two main "types" of meditation. Open monitoring and focused attention. In open monitoring, you allow thoughts and feelings to enter your mind, but give them no consideration, before letting them past and drift out of your mind again. Think of it rather like watching clouds float past on the breeze. Sounds and smells are recognized, but we are not reactive to them and like the thoughts allow them to pass without consideration. This form of meditation is practiced in Mindfulness Meditation, Vipassana and some forms of Taoist Meditation.

Focused attention meditation techniques involve focusing on one thing throughout the meditation. That thing can be an object, mantra, breath, visualization or a part of the body. It is exceedingly difficult, to begin with, to prevent thoughts and other outside influences from entering the mind. But these distractions become fewer as the focus is developed. This can take many years to achieve. Examples of this kind of meditation include Mantra Meditation, Samatha Meditation, Chakra Meditation, Zazen Meditation, Loving Kindness Meditation, Kundalini Meditation, Pranayama, Qigong and Sound Meditation.

Here we will look at some of the more common types of meditation so you can better understand them:

1. Mindfulness Meditation:

Mindfulness is an open monitoring technique. It's about being "in the moment," of being aware of, but not reactive to, what is going on around you. This includes not only your senses, sight, sound, touch, taste but also your thoughts and emotions.

2. Vipassana:

Another open monitoring technique. It involves seeing things as they really are. It requires the total elimination of all mental impurities in order to gain happiness and liberation. The focus is on the connection between the mind and the body through disciplined attention. This is observation based and educates you to understand your thoughts and feelings, helping you to free yourself from suffering, by increasing your awareness and self-control. With practice, you should achieve a mind that is well balanced and filled with love and compassion.

3. Taoist:

This is a Chinese tradition and is based on Taoism or Daoism philosophy. The emphasis is on living in harmony with nature, but Buddhist influences are also present.

This type of meditation is about inner energy generation, transformation and circulation. It is aimed at quieting the mind and body, the unification of body and spirit and finding inner peace. It can also have a focus of improving health and achieving longevity.

## 4. Mantra:

A mantra is a word, phrase or sound that is continually repeated during meditation. It is derived from Sanskrit and has two roots, man (which means mind or to think) and Trai, (which means to free from, protect or tool/instrument). Thus, mantra literally means a tool to free the mind.

This type of meditation is practiced by many contemplative traditions around the world and by many cultures and religions.

Mantras can be words that have meaning or just that give a great sound quality. They can be whole sentences long or short, or single words or even single syllables. Some mantras are recited by the meditator; some are listened to. They can be done fast when the aim is to create energy and enthusiasm or slowly to achieve peace and calmness. They can also be linked to other techniques such as breathing, visualizations or chakras.

5. Zazen:

Also known as Zen or Buddhist meditation, is based on "the four noble truths," these are:

To live means to suffer.

The origin of suffering is attachment.

The cessation of suffering is attainable.

The path to the cessation of suffering.

It means "seated meditation" in Japanese and comes from Chinese Zen Buddhism.

6. Loving Kindness (Metta) Meditation:

Metta means kindness, good will and benevolence and is a word from the Pali language in India. It originates from the Buddhist traditions in Tibet and Theravada. It is based on the idea of compassion meditation, with the aim to develop positive, loving, accepting emotions towards oneself and others.

7. Transcendental Meditation (TM):

This is a very specific form of mantra meditation and was developed in India by Maharishi Mahesh Yogi in 1955. It later gained popularity in the West during the late 60's and 70's by famous stars of the day such as The Beatles and The Beach Boys.

There are estimated to be over 5 million people practicing TM around the world. It has over 600 scientific papers about the benefits gained by TM.

However, TM can only be learned by going on a specialist course which is exceedingly expensive. It has been associated with cultish activities and there are doubts about the legitimacy of some or the research. For these reasons, it has many critics.

8. Yoga Meditation:

There are many different meditations associated with Yoga. Yoga in itself means union and is a form of exercise which uses physical postures, breathing and contemplative meditation.

It is believed to be the oldest tradition of meditation on Earth and has the widest variety of practices.

9. I Am:

This comes from the translation of the Sanskrit to investigate our true nature, atma vichara. Or Who am I? Finding the answer through meditation by developing an intimate self-knowledge. It gained great popularity in the 20th century due to an Indian sage called Ramana Maharshi. There is a movement that continues today, who were greatly inspired by his teachings, called the non-duality or neo-advaita movement. There are several different forms practiced, by contemporary teachers including Mooji, Adyashanti and Eckhart Tolle.

10. Qigong (Chi Kung):

This comes from Chinese and means "the cultivation of life energy." It's a mixture of exercise, meditation and martial art. Developed for the health of the mind and the body. It incorporates very slow body movements, regulate breathing and a strong inner focus.

Some Daoist practices also incorporate Qigong, but it is also used as a standalone method also.

11. Christian Meditation:

In the Eastern meditative traditions, meditations purpose is to gain "enlightenment." However, in Christian traditions, it is more usual for meditation to be practiced for other purposes, such as Deeper understanding, moral purification or intimacy with God. This can take several forms, including the silent repetition of word and sentences with a sacred meaning to focus devotion. Contemplation, which is reading and thinking about the teachings and events which occur in the Bible and silent meditation, also known as "sitting with God," where the mind heart and soul is focused on the presence of God.

12. Guided Meditation:

Great for beginners, guided meditation, is practiced using many of the different traditions already mentioned. A guide or teacher talks you through the meditation.

Because meditation requires you to be disciplined in finding the time and motivation, by joining a meditation group in your local area or even online, where you practice meditation together can help you get established.

Remember that you don't have to follow any specific form of meditation, you can just do what feels right for you and simply find a quiet place where you won't be disturbed. Set a timer for the length of time you want to meditate and then use either the open monitoring technique or the focused attention technique as you prefer.

## Chapter 15: 21 Days Action Plan To Gain Mindfulness

Once you go beyond the ability to live in the here and now, you'll be ready for more. If you want to try out your luck and earn mindfulness on your own you can try to do so following the 21 steps we are about to discuss.

You need to be aware of a couple of things though: gaining mindfulness it's not the same experience for everybody, that's the main reason why there are so many offerings and methods being sold out in the market today. Most of them are talking based on their own experience.

We, on the other hand, are taking a different approach by trying to offer a more universal take on mindfulness and giving you the option to choose the right measures to apply on a personal take to avoid fatigue, exhaustion or any of the negatives aspects that make these programs boring and tiresome.

We'll take on mindfulness one day at a time. Remember that every step is as flexible as you need it to be.

Day1

Try meditation. If it's your first time take into account everything we have talked about it in previous chapters, especially the indications offered in our introductory pages. Take a moment to do it the right way, try to reach a point where relaxation allows you to take a hold on every feeling of your body and the external influences don't distract you.

Persistence is the key to do it the right way, so you need to practice it every single day even if you go over the 21-day challenge mark. If you have practiced awareness previously by following the indications of the chapter about being here in the now you'll be able to achieve awareness of your body after a few tries. Since you are in the early stages of the program take a short time to begin your attempts. A ten-minute practice will suffice for now.

Day2

Clear your mind. After trying out meditation you'll probably come to the realization that it's very difficult to reach awareness if you don't have a clear head. The best thing you can do to try your luck with mindfulness on this day is to clear your head of good or bad thoughts. Make no judgments calls: your mind needs to be a clean slate to achieve mindfulness.

Day3

Make a connection. This day is specially designed to let yourself into the good thoughts that bring a connection, the ones that let your positive emotions run amok. Focus on these sensations and analyze the way they contribute to your emotional well-being. If you reach deep into every experience you are bound to find something that makes them more grounded into reality.

Day4

Practice with your senses. Every single nerve across your body will speak to you in a very different way. Try to put special attention on the senses that drive your anxiety levels higher or the one that gives the most displeasing experiences. Embrace every single feeling with a clear head and you'll be able to see the good and the bad on every single recollection. For this day try to process home life with this new approach. You'll probably notice just how different everything can be.

Day5

Let go, as simple as it sounds. You might not be ready to release your hold on some of the bad experiences you've had in your life, since you are very likely to feel they define you. However, this day is dedicated to putting your best effort into letting go all the baggage that you feel has shaped your character into something negative. Mindfulness doesn't require you to be a happy camper at all moments, but since you are trying your best to be a better person, you have to learn how to let go.

Day6

Take a day off. No, you are not doing it on purpose. If you are undertaking these steps with a clear head and in a serious way, you'll probably be emotionally exhausted and you need the rest. Take the day to realize how much you have advanced. Get a full view of your achievements and your setbacks. You are probably notice that your failures outweigh your victories but that doesn't mean you are failing at all. Just use your accumulated awareness to realize what needs improvement.

Day7

Retake the challenge. You'll notice how good it feels to be back and the little rest allows your newfound ability to concentrate to find focus more quickly. That's a victory right there! Concentrate on appreciating how your senses start handling every day experiences such as taking a simple shower or taking a run on a familiar part of town.

Day8

Apply what you have learned to situations created by your work environment. Try to gain awareness to process a mild conflict or something that requires effective thinking. Chances are you'll be able to handle yourself in a way that you didn't feel you could in the past. That's another victory right there. Don't feel discouraged if you are not lucky during the day, just get back home and practice your meditation.

Day9

Take a moment to notice how easy is getting for you to get into the mindset of meditating and getting control of your senses. By now the process should be automatic with those senses that you have chosen to practice more with. Try out your mindfulness at home and at work with specific experiences.

Day10

Manage your time. You probably haven't been paying attention to the time periods where you practice your mindfulness techniques. As a matter of fact we are willing to bet that you usually did it at the end of the day after work. Try to re-arrange your schedule and give everything the proper time it demands, even your meditation routine.

Day11

Take a moment to feel the state of your body before meditating. If you are still choosing to meditate after work and before bedtime you'll find that exhaustion probably make you less mindful of distractions, but it also means that your awareness will be affected, do your best to fit your meditation routine in other moments of the day if your working hours are flexible enough.

Day12toDay15

Time to test the new routine hours, you probably won't feel it this way at first but you are essentially training your senses to access mindfulness at will. Here is where all the time invested meditating starts to pay off, each time you are successful about perceiving something usual in a very different way, you are using the new state of your senses and this counts as a victory.

Day16

Test your abilities. On this day you will try out your awareness on every possible ground, your senses should have increased sharpness and your ability to see beyond the evident should be a bit more accurate than most. Your perception to your surroundings should also be a tad stronger than the one of your peers.

Day 17 and Day 18

While training your meditation techniques you should test your new ability to observe your inner self. Try out your newfound capability to connect with your senses, experience every sensation to the fullest and let your surroundings communicate whatever they have to tell you.

Day 19 and Day 20

Test your patience. Your new sensory experiences will probably overload your senses if you don't manage some control. To get there you need patience so you'll focus your meditation exercises into giving you all the patience you need to manage your senses the most optimal way.

Day21

We'll call this one "Consolidation Day" Sitting down to meditate should be an automatic exercise for you. Your senses are now giving you brand new experiences each day and you look forward to it. Each passing day you exert more control over every single experience you get from your environments. Congratulations! You are on the right path to success, and mindfulness is going to be a part of your life as long as you keep training for it.

## Chapter 16: Forgiveness

Like equanimity, learning to forgive means confronting the damage not forgiving does to us on the inside. Anger, resentment, jealousy, blame, and other negative emotions, are like a second hit we do to ourselves after receiving the first external blow. As with equanimity, when you are just beginning to meditate, it is best to start with a small issue so that you are not overwhelmed by your feelings. As you practice and get more powerful in your meditations, you can tackle bigger and bigger issues.

Forgiveness does not mean we excuse a behavior. Forgiveness means we make amends externally as we should—but also that we do not allow the negative emotions associated with what we have done to haunt our minds. Ask yourself: if a very close friend had done what you have done, how would you counsel them?

Would you suggest they stay haunted by what they had done for the rest of their lives—as we often do to ourselves? Of course not. You would tell them to make up for what they had done if they could, to accept inside that they made a mistake, and to promise themselves to do better in the future.

On the other hand, sometimes we feel other people have wronged us. It could be something simple, like being cut off in traffic. You grit your teeth and grip the wheel, and allow this anger to tear through the rest of your evening like an angry bull after a red cape. You are distracted during dinner, perhaps are not as attentive to your family as you should be, and grit your teeth while you try to watch some TV. Meanwhile, the person who cut you off has arrived home and is enjoying a relaxing evening, not having given the same situation that is troubling you a second thought.

Begin your forgiveness meditation as you do your equanimity meditation, but focusing on your posture, breath, and muscles until you are in a meditative state. Now, carefully move your attention from your breath to these thoughts:

I forgive myself...

For making mistakes, for not understanding, for hurting myself and others.

Keep focused on these thoughts. If you feel overwhelmed by negative emotions, temporarily return to focusing on your breathing until you once again feel centered in a meditative state. Then slowly return to these thoughts. If it feels too much for now, then simply focus on your breathing and end your meditation. Return to this issue in the future when you feel ready.

Now, center yourself on your breathing once again. When you are ready, move your attention to these thoughts:

I forgive you...

For not understanding, for making mistakes, for hurting me and others.

As with forgiving yourself, this practice can dredge up powerful emotions. If they become too strong, simply focus again on your breathing, acknowledging the emotions and allowing them to fade away as you focus on your breath. Return to the thoughts if you feel able, or end your meditation and return to them in the future.

**Chapter Summary.** These steps will help you learn how to forgive yourself and others, a necessary step in your journey to happiness:

Forgiving does not mean excusing.

Resentments and anger can be like a second insult that continues to harm us long after the first insult is long over.

Meditate to forgive yourself.

Meditate to forgive others.

Start small and work on larger issues as you grow in your abilities.

## Chapter 17: Simplify Your Work

Is it possible to get more done in a day? We all get the same twenty-four hours, so why does it seem like some people can do exponentially more? Some people are simply able to work smarter, not harder or longer. As we discussed in the last chapter, making some organizational changes to your office space may help streamline the process, but changing your mindset for work may do you one better.

Most of us process work as a means to run out the clock. If you are meant to work for eight hours a day, you figure out what you can do to make that time go by. This is the wrong way to think about it. Instead, ask yourself what are you capable of doing in that time? Raise your expectations of yourself, get more done, and get ahead without spending any more time.

Would you need to stay late at work if you crushed your daily to-do list, and had time to do the extra stuff your boss wanted done? Could you be insanely productive and still be home for dinner? This is all absolutely possible, and it's all a mind game.

First off, go in with a plan. At the end of each day, create a quick to-do list for the following morning. Get it all down on paper so that you may turn your brain off when your day is done. Do not look or think about that list again until the following morning. Be present and mindful in your life away from work if you are not in the office.

Going in fresh like this is vital. Plan to tackle that to-do list by noon. Instead of spreading out work to last the whole day, schedule different tasks in at different times. Perhaps that sales report has historically taken all day, but you procrastinated most of the time. Make a point to get it done in the hour it really takes. Focus all of your attention on that task until it is complete, without distraction. Regroup mid-day to eat, fuel up, and reassess the day. What's left on the to-do list, and what can you add for the afternoon? Five minutes left at the end of the day? Make that phone call you think can wait until tomorrow. What else can you knock off the list? We sprint to the finish, not slow as we see it coming into sight.

Scheduling is key. Schedule certain times to address emails and take phone calls. You don't need to check your email every time something new comes in. It is acting as a distraction to the task at hand, and every time you divert your attention, even for a minute, it takes another few minutes to refocus your attention on your task. Shut off pop-ups and reminders, silence your phone, and only address what you need to at any given time.

Perhaps the way you go about tasks needs to be addressed as well. Are you doing things the fastest and easiest way? Could you get more done if you simply streamlined your process? Would it be beneficial to outsource some of your work to someone else, so that you can focus on the real problems? Maybe you spend a good chunk of time scheduling clients at your office. Are there programs that could ease this process? Would hiring someone makes sense? Delegating works especially well if you push things you don't like to do, or aren't good at to someone who does like doing those things. Work together with your peers to help streamline everyone's work. Everybody wins.

Keep an open mind to how you do things. Before the invention of computers and the internet, people would keep records on paper, and for most businesses, would be a time-consuming process. Instead of living in the stone age, people adapted to use technology to take some of the workloads. This leaves time and energy for more important things and gives you the ability to get more done.

This situation is ideal for those who own their own businesses. These people are not punching the clock, they are getting work done. If necessary, they pull long shifts and work through the night to see their business succeed. These people don't pussyfoot around because they are not getting paid for every hour they put in. Procrastinating does not improve the bottom line. Working nine to five and getting an hour's worth of work done does not improve the business or bring in money.

No matter what type of business you are in, working for yourself or someone else, the same attitude will be beneficial. If you need to spend time at work, go ahead and get as much out of it as humanly possible. It is your time, you might as well feel productive, energetic and happy doing it. Hard work is always rewarded. Go above and beyond, leaving it all on the table each and every day. If you do work for yourself, get eight hours-worth of work done in five and enjoy the rest of your day as you see fit.

Is it possible to feel inspired to get after it every single day, day in and day out? Yes! Creating a positive work environment will mean you like going to work, interacting with your peers, and having a physical space that is conducive to work. Set up your space, so it is organized and easily worked in. Keep extra files out of sight and out of mind. Keep only what you are working on out on your desk.

Surround yourself with reminders of why you work so hard to get through those tough moments. If you work to keep your kids in a safe and happy home, be reminded of that by keeping their pictures close. If you work for yourself, have images or quotes that signify this dream at the ready. It is easy to get bogged down in the details, so it is important to constantly remind yourself why you are doing what you are doing. Consider this part of the interior design.

Last, but not least, work with your natural energy. If you tend to be a morning person, put the tough stuff on the list for a time you will be fresh. For example, if prospecting for new clients takes a lot out of you, get it done first thing when you are at your best. When you are a little drained, do some mindless work, like filing or answering emails for a little quiet time. Some of the best minds out there get up and start work insanely early, as this is when they are at their mental best. Play to your strengths.

## Chapter 18: Mindfulness For Empowerment

A model which explains the meaning behind every single decision we make, is shown below. This model shows why we do the things we do - from something as simple as eating a piece of chocolate cake, (when you know you really shouldn't) to the more extreme and unforgivable actions of murderers. Thoughts become actions, which yields a particular result and this either reinforces or breaks you free from a particular belief. These four principles; thoughts, actions, results and beliefs, all work in harmony to create a particular mindset. This can either be a positive mindset, or a negative mindset, they both occur from the same model.

Mindfulness allows you to target the very first and most important aspect of this model; thoughts. If you can be in control of your thoughts, it will have a cascading effect because all of these four principles interlink. Positive thoughts create positive actions, which brings positive results and this will help to reinforce a positive belief.

There's a certain level of responsibility and self-awareness that you will have to have in order to benefit from mindfulness. It's about being aware of your own internal dialogue (the thoughts and beliefs you have) and learning to take ownership and responsibility for it all, because it is a part of you. It's about not judging the thoughts you have, but rather seeing them in a peaceful manner, something which comes and goes like the soft, tides of the ocean.

The more you practice mindfulness, the greater sense of gratitude you will have. This is because you begin to realise just how precious each and every moment is. In a way, you step out of yourself and see that everything occurring in the present moment, is more peaceful than you think. It's our thoughts which can make everything seem so fast and worrisome, like when we are rushing to get things done. Mindfulness practice allows you to calm your mind, experience all that life has to offer right in this very moment and begin to see how each and every second is a gift.

Gratitude creates abundance

When you take the time, each and every day to be mindful of the present moment, you create gratitude and the power to be able to let go of your minds chaotic nature. This in turn, will create abundance in your life. By being grateful every day, you will find empowerment because you begin to live with more content and acceptance of your present reality.

As you can see, mindfulness can definitely help to empower you. You won't see yourself as a victim of your circumstances anymore, but rather the creator of your reality. I urge you to try mindfulness meditation. Try it in the morning before you go about your day, and also right before you go to sleep. It can take as little as 5 minutes all up daily, but the benefits you will obtain will be tremendous and absolutely life changing.

Finding the right mindfulness practice for you

In this book, we have gone over mindfulness meditation, but there many other ways that you can practice mindfulness. We are all different, so finding the right mindfulness practice for you is very important. You may find that meditation works for you and so you can stick with that, or you may be someone who needs something more dynamic and with more movement and physical expression.

Whatever your preference, there are many forms of mindfulness practice that you can try out and there is always one for everyone. It is completely individual and there is no right or wrong way to practice mindfulness. I recommend trying out all the practices we will go through in this chapter, in order to find one which you enjoy most.

1: Qigong

Qigong (pronounced: "chi gong") is an ancient Chinese practice, used to align the body, breath and mind for optimal health. Qigong is essentially an active form of meditation because it coordinates slow flowing movement, deep rhythmic breathing, and a calm meditative state of mind. This is a perfect form of mindfulness practice for those of you who find it very difficult to sit still. This is very true for a lot of us because most of us are thinking too much and when we sit still, thoughts bombard our consciousness. Qigong is perfect for this because it is a lot more dynamic and physically expressive.

2: Yoga

Yoga can also be a very useful practice to help you become more mindful as well as more flexible and physically healthy. There are many different forms of yoga that can be used to help alleviate stress, become more mindful of the present moment and overall live with a greater quality of life. With yoga, you practice poses which really require you to focus your awareness and attention to the present moment. You learn to listen to your body as you put yourself in physically demanding poses. You will find that yoga instructors repeatedly say to focus on your breathing. They are essentially saying to relax and relieve the tension within your body and mind; the essence of mindfulness practice.

3:Tai Chi

Tai Chi may look very similar to Qigong, i.e. the slow, meditative movements and 'soft' nature, however there are subtle differences. Tai Chi is actually a form of martial arts, whereas Qigong is primarily for healing. Try out both, they are very similar in their approach and practice. Both really emphasise a meditative and mindful state, by really focusing on every individual movement. Both practices require you to be present as much as possible. The experts within each field focus only on what they are doing in the present moment, rather than thinking ahead on what they are going to do next. This requires extreme focus. The saying; "empty your mind", is usually applicable and relevant to Chinese martial art and philosophy. It essentially means to be present and mindful of the here and now, by letting go of ego. This is the basis of mindfulness practice.

Whatever method you choose to approach your mindfulness practice, realise that you need to pick one that you feel is right for you. This takes a bit of experimenting and research. There are many more methods out there to help you become more mindful and it's up to you to find one that works for your individual needs.

Mindfulness is not just a practice, but it is deeply enriched in various cultures and their philosophies. It is essentially a way of life. Being able to step back and observe your internal condition is absolutely crucial to help you live a life with more peace and harmony. The majority of us have been so heavily engrained to always want more, or to search for something greater. It is only when you realise that all we have is the present moment that you can fully experience gratitude and true happiness. You essentially set yourself free. Free from the psychological prisons that only you can construct for yourself. Free from the ego self and free from self-inflicted pain and suffering.

## Chapter 19: Beginning Meditation

**Settle your mind.** It may take you a little bit of time to settle in and begin to detach from all the things going on in your life. Especially if you've had a stressful day, you may find yourself thinking about what happened or about things that need to happen in the future. You may feel your emotions stirring. All of this is okay. Notice that your mind is dancing, and let it dance for a bit as you settle in.

Keep in mind that it is okay if you feel a little strange about meditating. Just take a moment to identify the feelings you are having and then switch your focus to your physical position. Try to make yourself as comfortable as possible.

**Take some deep breaths**. Bring your awareness to your breath, noticing the inhalations and exhalations of each breath.[4] Feel how each breath flows in and out of your body, filling your lungs and then releasing through your throat and your mouth. Begin to lengthen and deepen each breath. Taking deep breaths helps settle and relax the mind and the body.

Observing your breath is also a mindfulness practice in itself. You can practice observing your breath for the entire length of the meditation.

**Realize that you are not your thoughts.** As you meditate, remind yourself that you have control over what thoughts and emotions you choose to engage.[6] When you notice thoughts or emotions coming up that you do not wish to engage, release them and choose not to put your focus onto them.

This insight can be helpful in realizing that you can change negative thoughts and that you can let them go.

Don't beat yourself up when you notice your mental stream of thoughts. Practice **letting go** of these mental experiences without judgment.

**Return to your breath.** Any time you get distracted by noises, thoughts, or anything, go back to observing your inhalations and exhalations. Any time you experience unpleasant thoughts or emotions, return your focus to your breathing.

When you focus on breathing, focus on neutrality. If thoughts come up while focusing on breathing, make sure you're maintaining the practice of not passing judgment on your thoughts, including on how you are practicing meditating. Judging yourself will interfere in your meditation session. Understand that it's common for people to get distracted or for thoughts to come up regarding their day.

Remember that meditation is not a performance

**Focus on the present.** One of the goals of mindfulness practices is to help you focus on the present moment. It's easy for your mind and emotions to jump to the future or back into the past, but your body is always in the present moment. This is why many mindfulness practices are body-driven. If you find your mind wandering often, return to your body, especially your breath. Try to focus only on the present moment.

## Chapter 20: Mindfulness Tips And Hacks

The following tips will help make the various forms of mindfulness—whichever you chose—part of your daily life:

Wake up mindfully

Your day should always begin on a mindful note. As you wake up, take in your immediate environment.

Take in the bed you lie on, try to recall any dream you had during the night, and see if you can trace its origin or implications. Sometimes we get divine direction and warnings that can help us have an idea of what awaits us during the day from dreams.

Meditate on whatever you can recall from your dreams, pray and give thanks to whatever deity you believe in for the gift of life, and take time to enjoy some deep breaths.

Acknowledge you are alive and be grateful for the gift of life, the gift of breath, the gift of a beautiful family and supportive friends, go through your mental list of everything you have going for you and everything you should be thankful for.

As you breathe in, feel the surge of fresh energy running through your body, and the cascade of negative energies and emotions leaving you as you breathe out.

Feel each breath, feel your abdomen rising with each inhalation and falling with each exhalation. If you can feel this, you are alive and living in the moment.

You can mindfully hit your legs on the floor, feel the sensation that runs through your body as you do so, and walk mindfully to the bathroom for a mindful cleanup or to your gym house/corner for some early morning mindful physical exercises.

Listen to people with deep attention and empathy

Whenever you engage someone in conversation and the person has something to say to you, simply listen without interrupting him or her with an argument, advice, or personal opinion. Let the person air his or her views and express his or her emotions and feelings. This will generate the empathy, compassion, and understanding you need to accept someone's emotion at any given moment as valid by putting yourself in the person's shoes. This is a sure way to improve your interpersonal relationships and give your character a boost.

Accept the world as it is and enjoy life while you still have it

It is natural to wish you were someone else or somewhere else at any difficult moment. Wishing our circumstances and the people in your life were not what they are at any moment cannot change your reality. You must come to a point where you understand that the world is fine as it is and every moment has a momentum and logic of its own, even with all the irregularities, imperfections, and angularities you have to live with.

Stop ranting about unfavorable situations and accept every moment as it is by embracing present realities and working to make the best out of them. This acceptance holds the key to your sanity and peace. This truth is one powerful antidote to depressive disorders and all of its symptoms.

Take some time off to relax

It is easy to decide you want to live more mindfully. However, making the decision and actually living a mindful life are not the same. Life is in a way that day-to-day realities will always seem to conspire against you and your decision to live life as it happens.

You will feel occasional tempers rising, tensions flying out of manageable proportion, and at such times, life might be anything but tranquil or peaceful, which makes concentrating on the moment and refusing to let worries, deadlines, bills, failing relationships, businesses, health, etc., distract you seem impossibility.

At such moments, all you need to stay mindful is to take time off everything and go relax somewhere serene. Just relax and breathe and everything will return to normal within a few minutes.

Set the 20 minutes goal

The 20 minutes technique helps a lot. Simply tell yourself you are going to live mindfully for the next 20 minutes. Observe the time and begin your mindful journey for the day. Let us say the time is 10:00 am, and you commit to engaging in a particular task mindfully for the next 20 minutes. At 10:20, you can commit to another mindful 20 minutes. This way, you will live your entire day in mindfulness and embark on your daily tasks mindfully.

## Conclusion

As you read the last few paragraphs of this book, take a moment to think of each word within this conclusion. If you do that, you really can practice mindfulness. Each word is placed in the sentence in an effort to persuade you that you have this wonderful power in your mind that you haven't yet unleashed. You go through the motions of living, but you are not conscious of what your life is.

It is a series of opportunities. Once you get the idea in your head that each moment may be the last, you begin to savor it more. By becoming more and more aware of your moments, they join together and make what become your future and your past, but the only one that you have any control over is **NOW**, in this very moment. How you learn is really dependent upon your life, as people from all over the world will have different rituals and habits. The important thing that everyone has in common is this moment. If it's wasted on criticism, if it's thrown away on regret, if it's ignored because of something your mind finds more pressing, it isn't lived to the full.

I would suggest that you go back through the chapters of this book and reread them with a more aware mind, taking each of the exercises set and trying them out for yourself. Make them a part of who you are. As you do, you will find that you become more open minded, and more able to accept who you are. It doesn't matter what religion you have because it doesn't come into it at all. What does come into it is belief in yourself, belief in what you experience each moment and belief that this moment leads on to the next.

It may seem minimalistic in nature, but it's the opposite. If you read a book with mindfulness in your lifestyle, you are more likely to take in more information. If you laugh or smile with a consciousness of doing it, you will feel the warmth radiate through you instead of merely showing on your face. Each opportunity and each moment that offers it is a celebration of life and once you start to celebrate it, you will be happier, more fulfilled and able to achieve much more because you are not letting your judgment get in the way of your own adaptability and acceptance.

www.ingramcontent.com/pod-product-compliance
Lightning Source LLC
Chambersburg PA
CBHW072011070526
44583CB00015B/1428